Dance
the
Country Western Way

Ya'akov Eden
Ball State University

KENDALL/HUNT PUBLISHING COMPANY
4050 Westmark Drive   Dubuque, Iowa 52002

Copyright © 1998 by Ya'akov Eden

ISBN 0-7872-4255-1

Printed in the United States of America
10 9 8 7 6 5 4 3 2 1

Contents

Name
111.2

Staple
in ABC order

Appendix D: Formations - Worksheets 161

Appendix E: Positions - Worksheets 165

Appendix F: Dance Worksheets 169

Acknowledgements

The most difficult task I encountered was in attempting to thank all the people who have been directly or indirectly involved in contributing to this book. First of all, I wish to thank my wife, Judy, who has been very patient, helpful, encouraging and tireless during the long hours of research and typing. The dancers have been a tremendous asset trying out all of these dances, putting up with my jokes and encouraging my efforts. Many heartfelt thanks go to Dr. John Reno, my School Chairperson, for his support and to the departmental secretaries, Sonja Pyles and Arlene Campbell, for their clerical assistance.

Special thanks to Beth Heim for her beautiful drawings and Pete Sampson for the musical notes.

I would also like to acknowledge the following Country Western dance teachers and specialists with whom I have had the privilege of studying with and/or teaching with: Daryll and Wanda Heath, Don and Shirley Hunt, Max Perry, Jo Thompson and Teresa White Borders.

And last but not least, I want to extend my gratitude to all of my students, past and present, for their uplifting spirit which has made teaching so enjoyable.

Introduction

Country Western dance is an integral part of an emerging American culture. In its origin, Country Western dancing had a few dances performed at special occasions in certain parts of the country. Today it has evolved into a social dance form embracing America and the world over.

Country Western dancing has moved from its original limited repertoire to a very broad selection of dance forms and styles. A variety of dance forms and styles has been developed, from line dancing to stylized couple dances.

In all Country Western dances we find a common denominator -- inward projection. People are dancing for their own benefit. Dancing can be found at numerous places such as clubs, bars and recreational facilities.

Each Country Western dance has a sequence of movements, a rhythmic structure and its own form. While all Country Western dances have the common bond of locomotion, there are subtle differences in the dynamics of performance. For example, there is no "Texan walk" and no "Californian run," but there are characteristic ways of doing them. These characteristic ways are the "style" of a dance or a group of dances from one area or people. It is in these different styles that the important differences among Country Western dances are found.

Music plays an important role in the enjoyment of the dance. The new rock style of country music has added to the popularity of Country Western dancing. It has a more upbeat style and has allowed for a greater variety of dance forms. This contemporary music has also attracted people from all walks of life, who were not necessarily fans of country music.

It is as important to execute the styling and mannerisms inherent in the dance as it is to be able to dance the steps and pattern sequences. Styling must be developed by the dancer or student to achieve the fullest enjoyment of the dance. The following are several points dancers could use in attempting to achieve the correct style in a dance or dances:

1. Study the background of the dance.
2. Develop an awareness of the characteristics of style.
3. Develop an understanding of the step patterns.
4. Be knowledgeable about the formations and positions.

It is my philosophy that no culture can be learned fully unless one learns to understand the music, dance and art of a culture. Country Western dancing is truly an American social dance form which is beautiful and here to stay.

Ya'akov Eden
June 1997

Abbreviations

Bkwd	-	**Backward**
CCW	-	**Counter Clockwise**
CTS	-	**Counts**
CW	-	**Clockwise**
Diag	-	**Diagonal**
Fwd	-	**Forward**
L	-	**Left**
LOD	-	**Line of Direction or Dance**
R	-	**Right**
RLOD	-	**Reverse Line of Direction or Dance**

COUNTRY WESTERN DANCE FUNDAMENTALS

Country Western Fundamentals

Country Western Dance, as other dance forms, consists of four main elements: rhythm, basic movements, formations and positions. Each of these categories will be discussed in its relation to Country Western Dance. The uniqueness of Country Western Dance is the manner in which these elements are performed, giving each dance its own style. Even though a walking step by definition is true to all mankind, it is the styling that each dance or element possesses that gives it a different look.

Time

Rhythm is an essential part of a Country Western dance. It is to rhythm that we execute every movement. The fundamentals of rhythm are as follows:

<u>Notes</u>

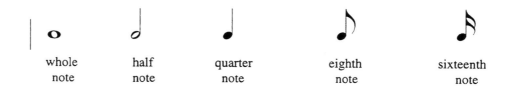

| whole note | half note | quarter note | eighth note | sixteenth note |

Measures and Time Signatures

A measure is a length of time in music which is determined by its time signature. For example, in a time signature of 4/4 there are four quarter notes to one measure; in a 3/4 time signature there are three quarter notes to a measure.

Time Signatures Used in Country Western Dance

4/4   Four beats to a measure. The accent is on the first beat.

3/4   Three beats to a measure. The accent is on the first beat.

2/4   Two beats to a measure. The accent is on the first beat.

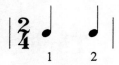

6/8   Six beats to a measure. The accent is on the first beat.

6/8   When played in triplets, it will sound like 2/4. The accent is on the first and fourth beats.

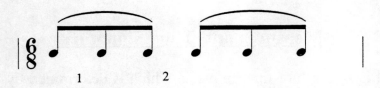

4

Basic Locomotor Movements
Basic Non-Locomotor Movements
Single Action Movements

Basic movements can be described in a progressive order, such as: locomotor movements, non-locomotor movements, basic steps and dance (or part of a dance).

Basic Locomotor Movement

These are single action movements where a shift of weight takes place. Basic locomotor movements include the following: Walk, Run, Leap, Hop, Jump. Some movement exploration experts consider the Skip, Slide and Gallup as basic locomotor movements even though they have two actions each.

Walk - Transfer of weight from one foot to the other, while keeping in touch with the ground at all times.

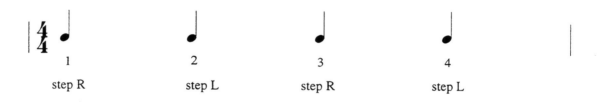

Run - Transfer of weight from one foot to the other while both feet are momentarily off the ground.

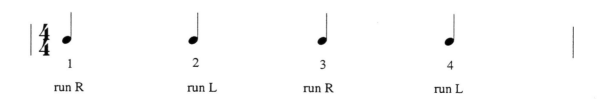

Leap - Similar to run. Taking off with a given foot and landing on the opposite while momentarily sustaining the body in the air in an arc-like motion.

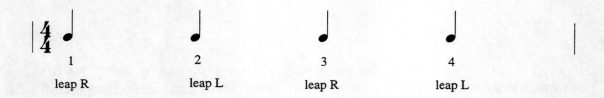

Hop - Taking off with a given foot and landing on the same.

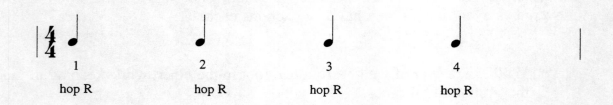

Jump - Taking off with both feet and landing on both. Can be done by taking off with one foot and landing on both or taking off with both feet and landing on one.

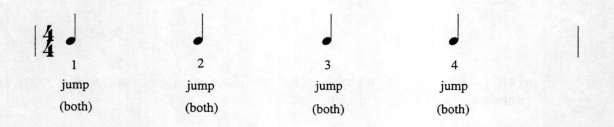

Even though the next three movements have more than one action, they are considered by some movement exploration experts as basic locomotor movements.

Skip - Hop on Left, step with the Right in an uneven rhythm. Can be done with either foot.

| & | 1 | & | 2 |
| hop L | step R | hop R | step L |

Slide and Gallup - These two movements are similar. The difference is in the direction of the movement. The gallup moves forward, the slide moves to the side. Step forward or sideways on a given foot and leap with the opposite foot landing beside the original stepping foot.

Slide - Step with the Right to the Right and leap with the Left, landing beside the Right. Can be done with either foot to both sides.

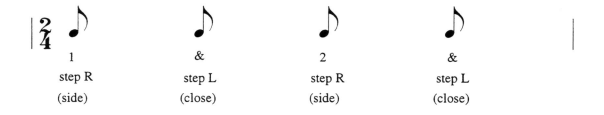

1	&	2	&
step R	step L	step R	step L
(side)	(close)	(side)	(close)

Gallop - Step Right forward and leap with Left, landing beside the Right. Can be done with either foot.

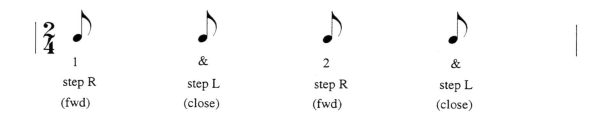

1	&	2	&
step R	step L	step R	step L
(fwd)	(close)	(fwd)	(close)

Basic Non-Locomotor Movement

These are single action movements of a given body part without shift of weight. Basic Non-Locomotor movements include the following: Bend, Brush, Bump, Clap, Head Roll, Hip Isolation, Hitch, Hook, Kick, Pivot, Scuff, Shimmy, Slap, Squat, Stomp Up, Stretch, Swing, Swivel, Tap, Thrust, Touch, Twist.

Bend - Bend any joint, such as: knee, elbow or wrist.

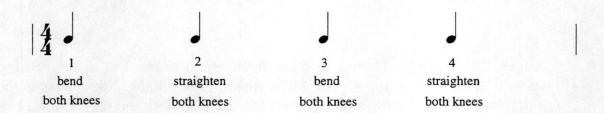

1	2	3	4
bend	straighten	bend	straighten
both knees	both knees	both knees	both knees

Bounce - An elevation of the body by raising the heels off the ground and lowering the heels. Both actions are usually done in one count.

&	1	&	2
heels	heels	heels	heels
(up - down)	(up - down)	(up - down)	(up - down)

Brush - A movement where the toes or ball of the foot come in contact with the floor. Swing any leg in any direction while touching the floor with the toes or ball of foot. Can be done with either foot in any direction.

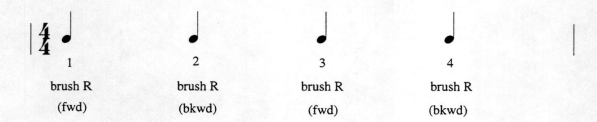

1	2	3	4
brush R	brush R	brush R	brush R
(fwd)	(bkwd)	(fwd)	(bkwd)

8

Bump - Move a hip in any given direction with an accent.

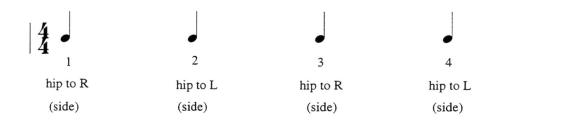

1	2	3	4
hip to R	hip to L	hip to R	hip to L
(side)	(side)	(side)	(side)

Clap - Strike hands together in any manner asked for.

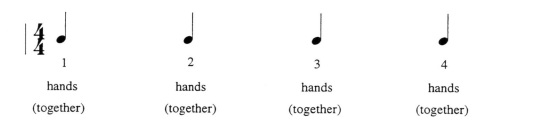

1	2	3	4
hands	hands	hands	hands
(together)	(together)	(together)	(together)

Head Roll - Turn the head in any given direction in a circular manner.

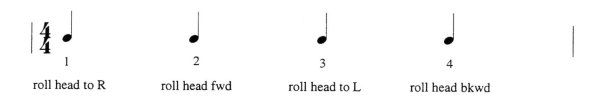

1	2	3	4
roll head to R	roll head fwd	roll head to L	roll head bkwd

Hip Isolation - Move a given hip in any given direction, while opposite knee is bent.

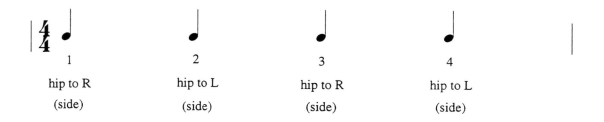

1	2	3	4
hip to R	hip to L	hip to R	hip to L
(side)	(side)	(side)	(side)

Hitch - Lift the knee of the inactive leg, bending knee in a 45 degree angle. For example, step Right forward while lifting the Left leg with a bent knee. Can be done with either leg.

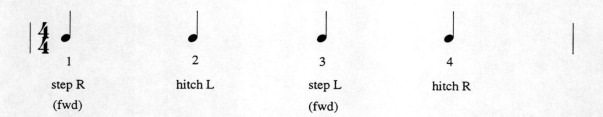

1	2	3	4
step R	hitch L	step L	hitch R
(fwd)		(fwd)	

Hold - Hold a position for a given amount of time.

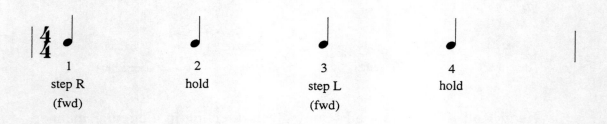

1	2	3	4
step R	hold	step L	hold
(fwd)		(fwd)	

Hook - Swing the Right heel across the Left shin. Can be done with either foot.

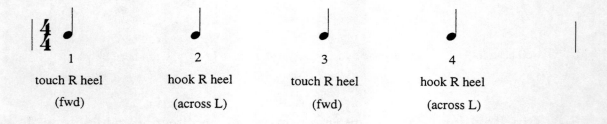

1	2	3	4
touch R heel	hook R heel	touch R heel	hook R heel
(fwd)	(across L)	(fwd)	(across L)

Kick - A sharp swinging action of the leg from the knee down. Usually in a forward direction. Can be done with either foot in any given direction.

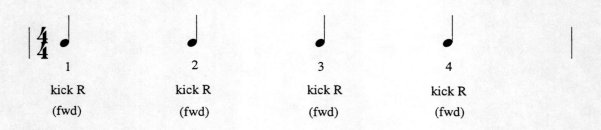

1	2	3	4
kick R	kick R	kick R	kick R
(fwd)	(fwd)	(fwd)	(fwd)

Pivot - A turning motion on the ball of the foot that has the weight. Step Right forward, turn on the ball of the Right in any given direction and maintain the weight on the Right. Can be done with either foot in any direction.

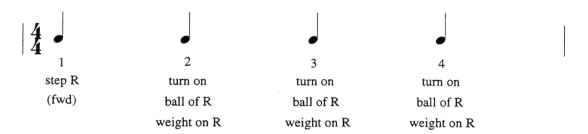

1	2	3	4
step R	turn on	turn on	turn on
(fwd)	ball of R	ball of R	ball of R
	weight on R	weight on R	weight on R

Scuff - A movement where the heel comes in contact with the floor. Strike the floor with the heel in a forward motion without a shift of weight.

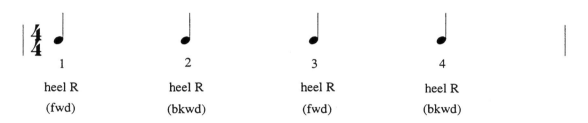

1	2	3	4
heel R	heel R	heel R	heel R
(fwd)	(bkwd)	(fwd)	(bkwd)

Shimmy - A side to side or forward and back isolation of the shoulders.

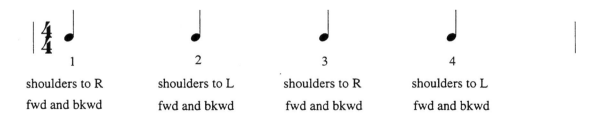

1	2	3	4
shoulders to R	shoulders to L	shoulders to R	shoulders to L
fwd and bkwd	fwd and bkwd	fwd and bkwd	fwd and bkwd

Slap - Striking a body part with the hand.

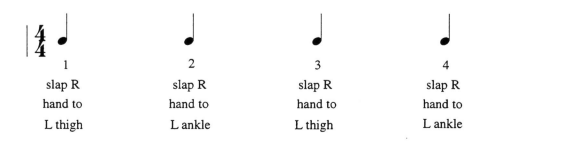

1	2	3	4
slap R	slap R	slap R	slap R
hand to	hand to	hand to	hand to
L thigh	L ankle	L thigh	L ankle

Squat - Changing level (down) by bending the knees.

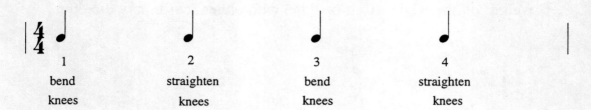

1	2	3	4
bend knees	straighten knees	bend knees	straighten knees

Stomp Up - An accented step without shifting weight to the active foot. Step Right beside the Left with an accent, without shifting weight to Right. Can be done with either foot.

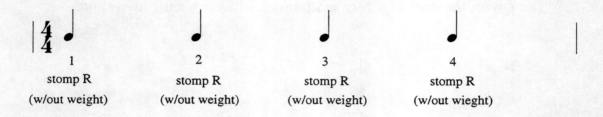

1	2	3	4
stomp R (w/out weight)	stomp R (w/out weight)	stomp R (w/out weight)	stomp R (w/out wieght)

Swing - A forward or backward movement of any leg or arm.

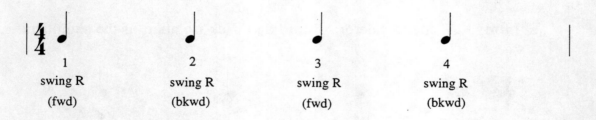

1	2	3	4
swing R (fwd)	swing R (bkwd)	swing R (fwd)	swing R (bkwd)

Swivel - Turning of heel or toes from side to side on the ball or balls of the feet or heels.

Heel Swivels

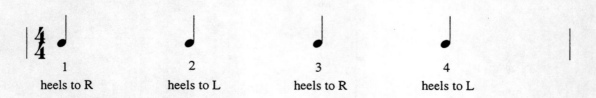

1	2	3	4
heels to R	heels to L	heels to R	heels to L

12

Toe Swivels

1	2	3	4
toes to R	toes to L	toes to R	toes to L

Tap - See Touch.

Thrust - A sharp forward or backward isolation of the pelvis or hip.

Pelvis Thrust

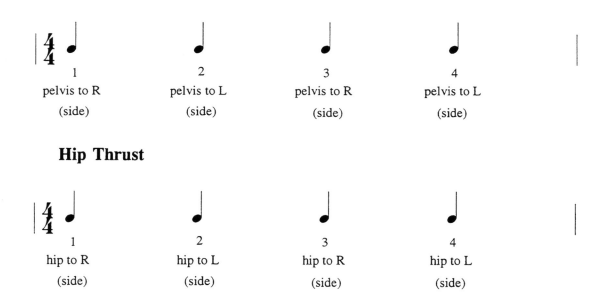

1	2	3	4
pelvis to R	pelvis to L	pelvis to R	pelvis to L
(side)	(side)	(side)	(side)

Hip Thrust

1	2	3	4
hip to R	hip to L	hip to R	hip to L
(side)	(side)	(side)	(side)

Touch - Touch the floor with the heel or toe without shifting of weight. Can be done with either foot in any direction.

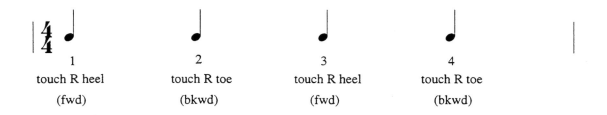

1	2	3	4
touch R heel	touch R toe	touch R heel	touch R toe
(fwd)	(bkwd)	(fwd)	(bkwd)

Single Action Movements

These are single action movements (not basic locomotor) where a shift of weight takes place. These movements are not considered to be Basic Steps. They include the following: Chug, Cross, Lift, Lock, Lunge, Scoot, Stomp, Swivel, Unwinding Turn.

Chug - A movement involving scooting on the feet without leaving the ground. Scoot forward and backward in one count. Can be done on one or two feet.

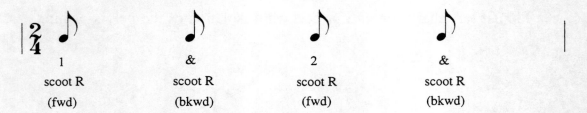

1	&	2	&
scoot R	scoot R	scoot R	scoot R
(fwd)	(bkwd)	(fwd)	(bkwd)

Cross - Step with one foot in front of the opposite foot. Can be done with either foot in any direction.

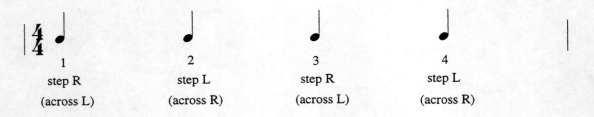

1	2	3	4
step R	step L	step R	step L
(across L)	(across R)	(across L)	(across R)

Lift - Elevation of the heels off the floor and lowering the heels to the floor. Can be done in one or two counts.

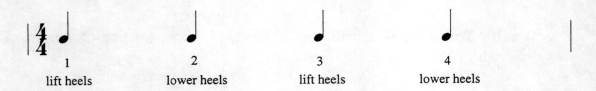

1	2	3	4
lift heels	lower heels	lift heels	lower heels

Lock - Step with a given foot forward and around (outside) the opposite foot, giving it a feeling of locking the feet together.

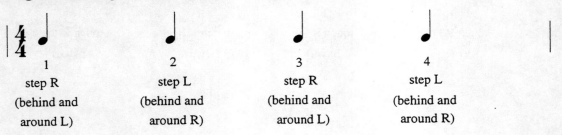

1	2	3	4
step R	step L	step R	step L
(behind and around L)	(behind and around R)	(behind and around L)	(behind and around R)

14

Lunge - A wide step to a given side. The body leans in the direction of the active foot. The opposite leg is straight.

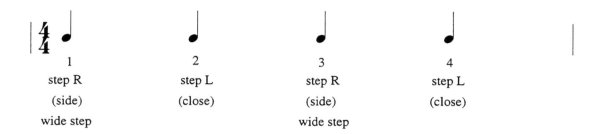

Scoot - A movement forward on the active foot, similar to a hop without leaving the ground.

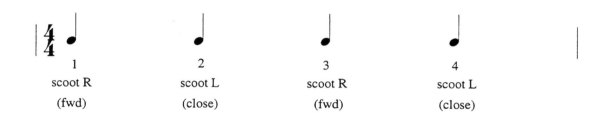

Stomp - An accented step, with a shift of weight.

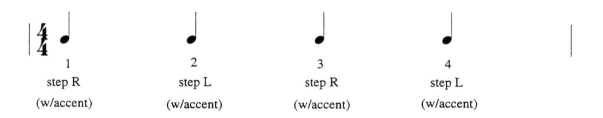

Unwinding Turn - Feet in a crossed position (one foot across the opposite), turn on the balls of the feet to uncross the legs.

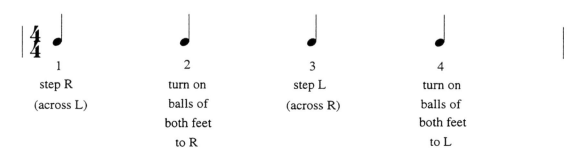

15

Basic Steps

These are any combination of one or more Locomotor and/or Non-Locomotor Movements. They include the following: Balance, Ball Change, Boogie Walk, Break, Break Turn, Butterflies, Caribbean Walk, Cha Cha, Charleston, Coaster, Cross Rock Step, Fan, Front Sailor, Grapevine, Heel Splits, Hook Step, Jazz Box, Jumping Jack, Kick Ball Change, Military Turn, Military Pivot Turn, Out-Out-In-In, Paddle Turn, Pivot, Polka, Polka Turn, Prance, Promenade, Reel, Rock, Rocking Chair, Rolling Vine, Running Man, Sailor Shuffle, Sailor Step, Shuffle, Side Cross, Star, Step Behind, Step Hop, Strut, Sway, Syncopated Reel, Tcherkessia Step, Triple Step, Turn, Twinkle, Two-Step, Vine, Waltz, Waltz Balance, Waltz Turns, Weave.

Balance - A stationary Basic Step which moves in opposite directions. Step Right to Right, step Left to Left. Can be done with either foot from side to side or forward and backward.

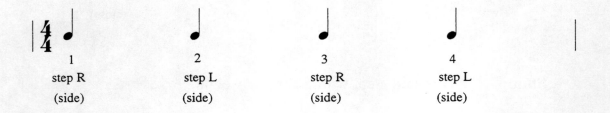

Ball Change - Step on the ball of the active foot then shift weight to the opposite foot. At times used as a turning movement.

Boogie Walk - Walking steps, stepping across the supporting foot and turning the active knee in.

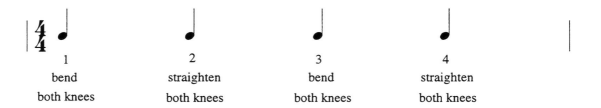

1	2	3	4
bend	straighten	bend	straighten
both knees	both knees	both knees	both knees

Break - Step back on the first step and shift weight forward to the opposite foot. It is the ending sequence when doing the East Coast Swing.

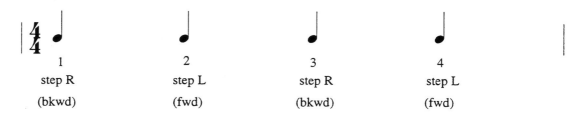

1	2	3	4
step R	step L	step R	step L
(bkwd)	(fwd)	(bkwd)	(fwd)

Break Turn - Step forward with one foot, turn a 1/2 turn on the supporting foot and shift weight to the opposite foot.

Right Break Turn - Step Left forward and turn a 1/2 turn to Right.

Left Break Turn - Step Right forward and turn a 1/2 to Left.

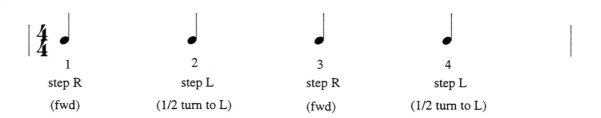

1	2	3	4
step R	step L	step R	step L
(fwd)	(1/2 turn to L)	(fwd)	(1/2 turn to L)

Butterflies - See Heel Splits

Caribbean Walk - Side steps, isolating a hip by bending the opposite knee. When turning the Right knee in, the Left hip will move to the Left.

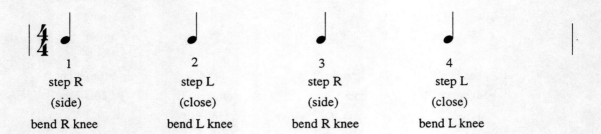

1	2	3	4
step R	step L	step R	step L
(side)	(close)	(side)	(close)
bend R knee	bend L knee	bend R knee	bend L knee

Cha Cha - A Ballroom Basic Step. In Ballroom, the Cha Cha is a Basic Step with five steps to it. The last three steps in the Cha Cha sequence are described here. In a Q,Q,S rhythm, step Right to Right, step Left beside Right, step Right to Right.

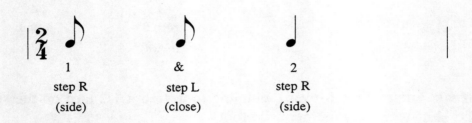

1	&	2
step R	step L	step R
(side)	(close)	(side)

Charleston - A four count movement. Step Right forward, Kick Left forward, Step Left backward, Touch Right backward. Can be done with either foot.

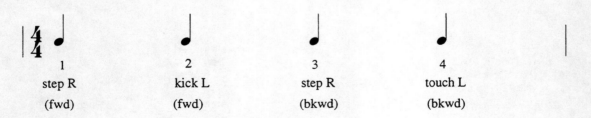

1	2	3	4
step R	kick L	step R	touch L
(fwd)	(fwd)	(bkwd)	(bkwd)

Coaster - A three step sequence done in a Q,Q,S, rhythm. Step Right backward, step Left beside Right, step Right forward. Can be done with either foot.

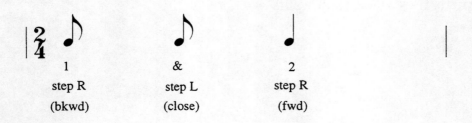

1	&	2
step R	step L	step R
(bkwd)	(close)	(fwd)

Cross Rock Step - A three step sequence done in a Q,Q,S, rhythm. Step Right across Left, step Left backward, step Right to Right. Can be done with either foot to both sides.

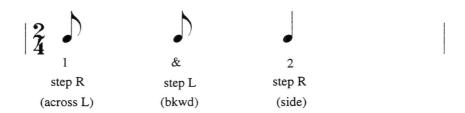

1	&	2
step R	step L	step R
(across L)	(bkwd)	(side)

Fan - A two action step. Turn Right toes to Right, return Right toes to place. Can be done with either foot in any direction.

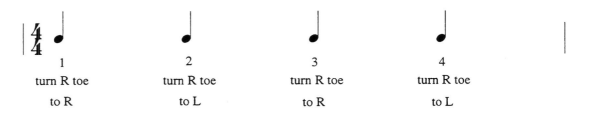

1	2	3	4
turn R toe	turn R toe	turn R toe	turn R toe
to R	to L	to R	to L

Grapevine - One foot steps to the side while opposite foot steps in front or behind. Example: Step Right to Right, step Left across Right, step Right to Right, step Left behind Right. Can be done with either foot in any direction.

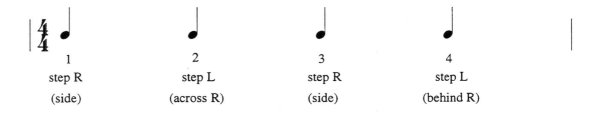

1	2	3	4
step R	step L	step R	step L
(side)	(across R)	(side)	(behind R)

Heel Splits - Turn heels out and return heels to place.

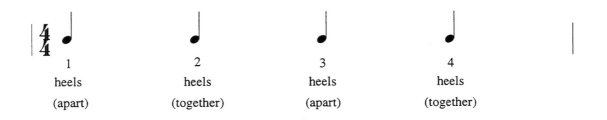

1	2	3	4
heels	heels	heels	heels
(apart)	(together)	(apart)	(together)

Hook Step - This is a four count Basic Step. Touch Right heel forward, Swing Right heel across Left shin, Touch Right heel forward, step Right beside Left. Can be done with either foot.

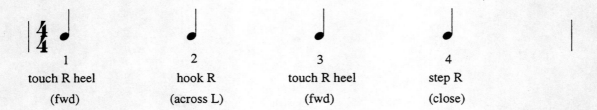

1	2	3	4
touch R heel	hook R	touch R heel	step R
(fwd)	(across L)	(fwd)	(close)

Jazz Box - Jazz Boxes can be executed in manydifferent ways, and they can take three, four or five counts. It all depends on the type asked to perform in each dance. Basically the Jazz Box looks as follow: Step Right across Left, step Left backward, step Right to Right, step Left beside Right. Can be done with either foot in any direction.

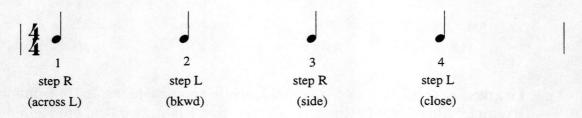

1	2	3	4
step R	step L	step R	step L
(across L)	(bkwd)	(side)	(close)

Jumping Jack - Jump and land with feet apart, Jump and land with feet together.

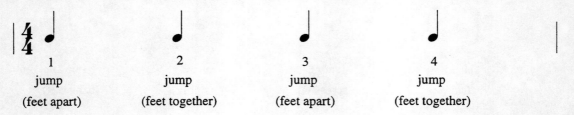

1	2	3	4
jump	jump	jump	jump
(feet apart)	(feet together)	(feet apart)	(feet together)

Kick Ball Change - A three step sequence done in a Q,Q,S, rhythm. Kick Right forward, step backward on ball of Right beside Left, step Left forward. Can be done with either foot.

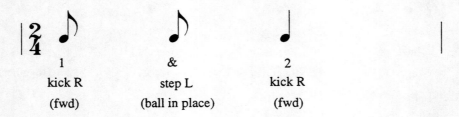

1	&	2
kick R	step L	kick R
(fwd)	(ball in place)	(fwd)

Military Turn (1/4) - Pivot on the heel of one foot and on ball of the opposite foot and turn a 1/4 turn. If turning to the Left, pivot on the Left heel and ball of Right. Can be done to either side.

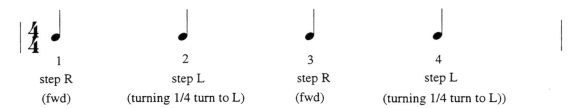

1	2	3	4
step R	step L	step R	step L
(fwd)	(turning 1/4 turn to L)	(fwd)	(turning 1/4 turn to L))

Military Pivot Turn (1/2) - See Break Turn

Out-Out-In-In - A Basic Step done in half-time. Step Right to Right, step Left to Left (end with feet shoulder width apart), step Right to Left, step Left beside Right (feet are now together).

&	1	&	2
step R	step L	step R	step L
(to R)	(to L)	(to R)	(to L)

Paddle Turn (1/4) - Step Right forward leading with the Right hip and shoulder, pivot on Right to Left turning a 1/4 turn to Left. Shift weight to Left.

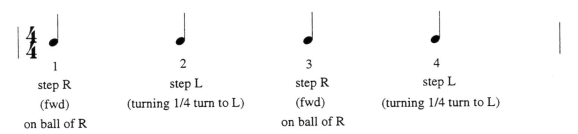

1	2	3	4
step R	step L	step R	step L
(fwd)	(turning 1/4 turn to L)	(fwd)	(turning 1/4 turn to L)
on ball of R		on ball of R	

Pivot - Turning on a stationary point. A given movement will be done in a circular manner without going away from that point. For example, when turning, the Right foot will remain in the same spot while the Left foot will travel around.

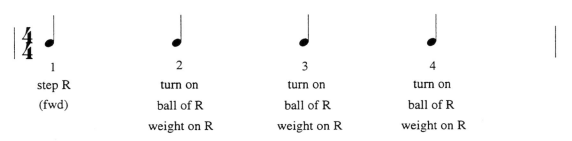

1	2	3	4
step R	turn on	turn on	turn on
(fwd)	ball of R	ball of R	ball of R
	weight on R	weight on R	weight on R

Polka - This description is of the traditional Polka step. In Country Western dance the Polka is actually a Shuffle without the Hop. The Polka consists of a hop and a fast Two Step (Shuffle). For example, Hop on Left, fast Two-Step (Shuffle) with Right. Can be done with either foot in any direction.

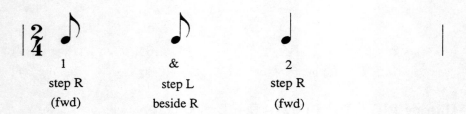

Polka Turn - Partners in Shoulder-Waist Position or Closed Position, execute a Polka Step while turning a 1/2 turn to Right during the Hop.

Prance - A stylized run. As one foot runs, the opposite is lifted with a raised knee and pointed toes.

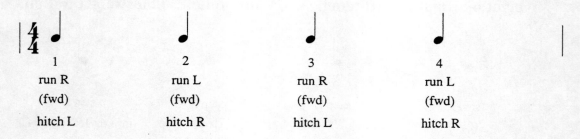

Promenade - It is both a position (Skaters Position) and a movement. As a movement, partners join hands in Promenade (Skaters) Position and walk around the circle or dance floor.

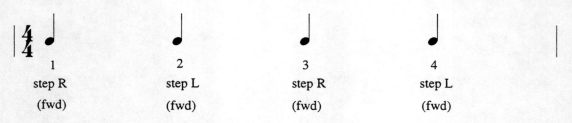

22

Reel - The Reel is originally an Irish Basic Step. Step Right behind Left, step Left behind Right, step Right behind Left, step Left behind Right and so on.

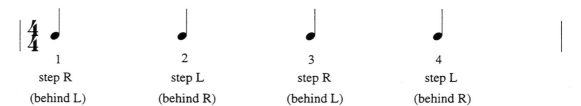

Syncopated Reel- The same as the Reel but done in half time.

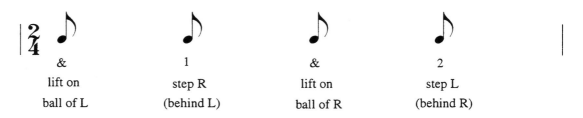

Rock - A Basic Step where weight is shifted in opposite directions. Step Right forward, step Left backward. Can be done with either foot in any direction. When beginning backward it is also called a Break.

Backward Rock (Break)

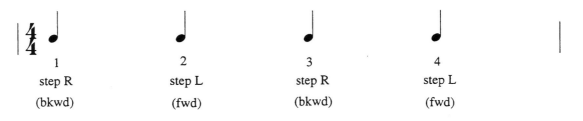

Forward Rock

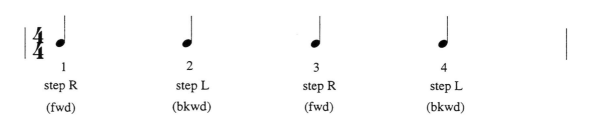

Side Rock

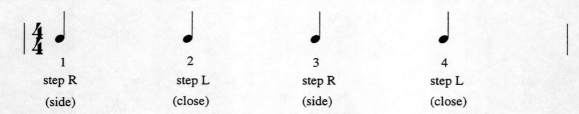

Rocking Chair - A four count step. Step Right forward, step Left backward, Step Right backward, step Left forward. Can be done with either foot in any direction.

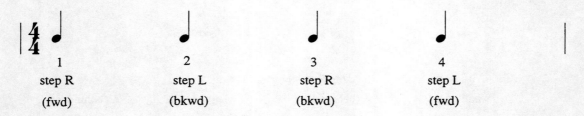

Running Man - This is a more contemporary Basic Step. It is done with two actions to one count. Step Right forward, Chug (hop) Right Backward while hitching Left, Step Left forward, Chug (hop) Left backward while hitching Right.

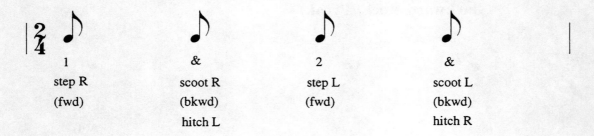

Sailor Step - A three step sequence done in a Q,Q,S, rhythm. Step Right behind Left, step Left to Left, step Right to Right (using very small steps). Can be done with either foot.

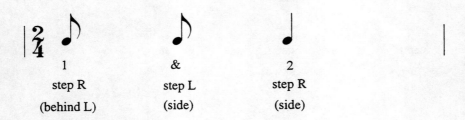

24

Front Sailor - A three step sequence done in a Q,Q,S, rhythm. The step is the same as the basic Sailor step, except step across in front rather then behind. Step Right across Left, step Left to Left, step Right to Right, (done with very small steps). Can be done with either foot.

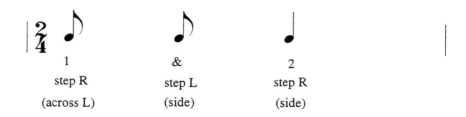

Sailor Shuffle - A three step sequence done in a Q,Q,S, rhythm. The step is the same as the basic Sailor step but it travels backward rather than remaining stationary. Step Right behind Left, step Left backward, step Right backward, (using very small steps). Can be done with either foot.

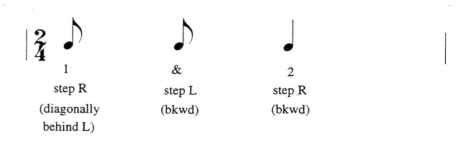

Shuffle - A three step sequence done in a Q,Q,S rhythm. It is described as a step together step. Step Right to Right, step Left beside Right, step Right to Right. Can be done with either foot in any direction.

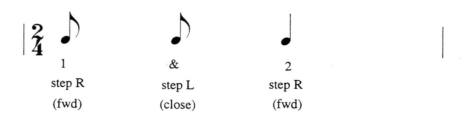

Side Cross - Step Right to Right, step Left across Right. Can be done with either foot in any direction.

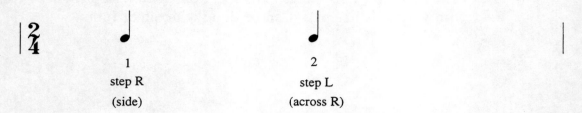

Star (Slap Leather) - This is one of many versions of the step. Touch Right heel Forward, touch Right toes to Right, touch Right toes behind Left, touch Right toes to Right and so on. In each dance the description will be clear as to how many touches take place. Can be done with either foot in any direction.

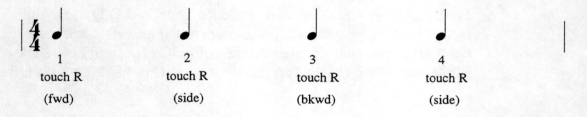

Step Hop - Step Right and hop on it. Can be done with either foot in any direction.

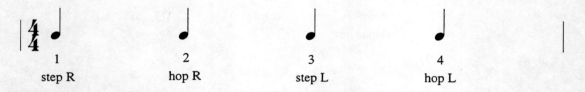

Strut - A stylized walk, leading with the heel or toes and transferring the weight to the whole foot. Usually takimg two counts. Can be done with either foot, forward or backward.

Toe & Heel Strut

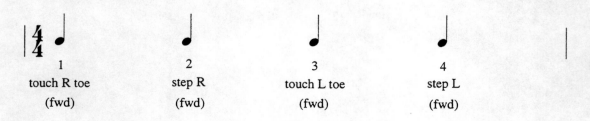

Heel & Toe Strut

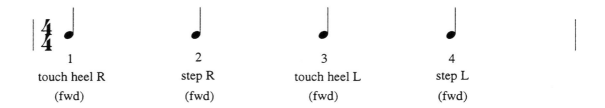

1	2	3	4
touch heel R	step R	touch heel L	step L
(fwd)	(fwd)	(fwd)	(fwd)

Sway - Shift of weight from one foot to the other while body sways from side to side. Standing with feet apart. Can be done in any direction.

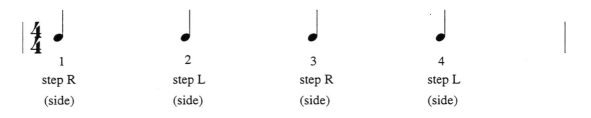

1	2	3	4
step R	step L	step R	step L
(side)	(side)	(side)	(side)

Tcherkessia Step - See Rocking Chair (This is the Folk Dance name for the step).

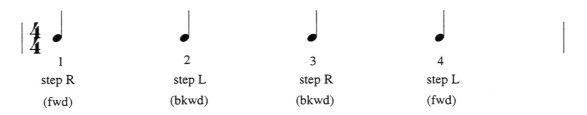

1	2	3	4
step R	step L	step R	step L
(fwd)	(bkwd)	(bkwd)	(fwd)

Triple Step - A Basic Step in the Triple Lindy or East Coast Swing. A three step sequence done in a Q,Q,S, rhythm. Step Right to Right, step Left beside Right, step Right to Right. Can be done with Left to Left.

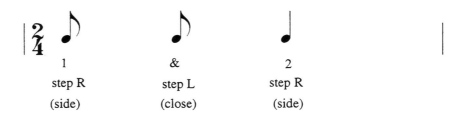

1	&	2
step R	step L	step R
(side)	(close)	(side)

Turn - A movement that progresses in a circular direction. You can turn a 1/4 turn, a 1/2 turn or a full turn. The type of turn to be executed will be specified in each dance.

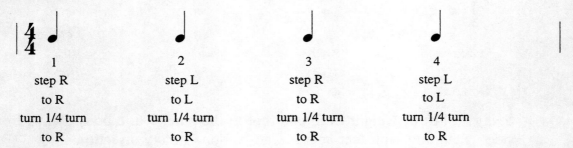

1	2	3	4
step R	step L	step R	step L
to R	to L	to R	to L
turn 1/4 turn	turn 1/4 turn	turn 1/4 turn	turn 1/4 turn
to R	to R	to R	to R

Twinkle - See Waltz Twinkle

Two-Step - See Shuffle

Vine - In Country Western Dance the Vine is the name used for the Grapevine. It has become a standard for three steps and a forth action that could be a Touch, Scoot, Hitch Kick and so on. Step Right to Right, step Left behind Right, step Right to Right, touch Left beside Right. It can be done with either foot in any direction.

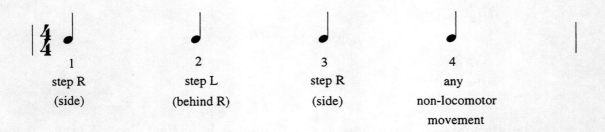

1	2	3	4
step R	step L	step R	any
(side)	(behind R)	(side)	non-locomotor
			movement

Rolling Vine (full turn) - The same as the basic Vine but completing a full turn with the three steps. Can be done with either foot in any direction.

Syncopated Vine (double time) - The same as the basic Vine but each action done to a half beat. Can be done with either foot in any direction.

Waltz (Basic) - Step Right forward, Step Left beside Right, step Right beside Left. Can be done with either foot in any direction.

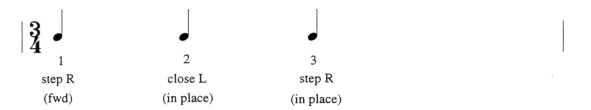

Waltz - Balance - Step Right to Right, step Left beside Right. Step Right beside Left. Can be done with opposite footwork in any direction.

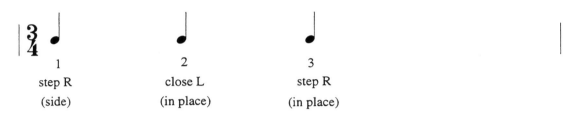

Waltz - Half Box - Step Right forward, Step Left to Left, Step Right beside Left. Can be done forward or backward with either foot.

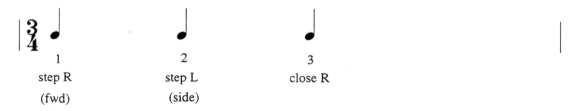

Waltz Turns

Waltz - Box Turn (1/4 turn) - A basic turn in the English Waltz. When executing the Right turn (CW): step Right forward, step Left to Left while turning a 1/4 turn to Right (CW), step Right beside Left. When the Left foot is the active foot, the turn will be done as follow: Step Left backward, Step Right to Right while turning a 1/4 turn to Right, step Left beside Right.

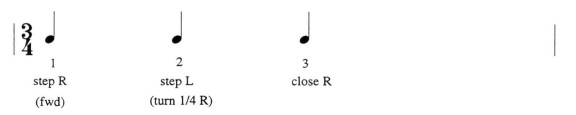

Waltz - Half Turn - The same as in the Box Turn, except turn a 1/2 turn.

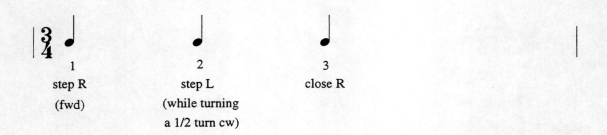

1	2	3
step R	step L	close R
(fwd)	(while turning	
	a 1/2 turn cw)	

Waltz - Twinkle - a Basic Step used in the Waltz. Step Right across Left, step Left beside Right, step Right beside Left. Can be done with either foot in any direction.

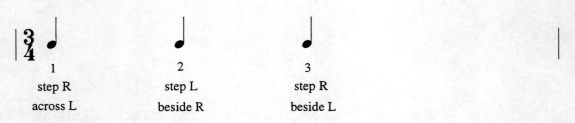

1	2	3
step R	step L	step R
across L	beside R	beside L

Weave - See Grapevine

Formations

Circle

Contra

Couple

**Couples in a
Single Circle**

Double Circle

Line (Scatter)

33

Positions

Butterfly

Buzz (Swing)

Closed

Conversation

Open

Promenade

Shoulder Waist

Simple Hold (V)

Varsouvienne
(Sweetheart or Side by Side)

COUNTRY WESTERN DANCE TEACHING METHODS

Methodology

The methodology of teaching Country Western dance embodies certain elements which will be discussed in this chapter. Dealing with different terms which may be foreign to most requires preparation, knowledge of Basic Steps, terminology, planning, styling, progression and modification.

There are many approaches to teaching Country Western dance. When deciding on the best way to teach a dance, keep in mind that Country Western dance is a social activity, an avenue for folks to relate, socialize, gain knowledge of other steps and dances and most important, to develop a lifetime activity which is a positive and enriching experience.

Remember that movement is essential in life. A person walks or runs from place to place. When approaching a puddle the only way to cross it would be to jump or leap over it. And if a foot were injured, a person might resort to hopping. These examples illustrate quite clearly that people use the basic locomotor movements in their everyday life. This being the case, everyone should be able to dance. In order for people to learn to dance, the teacher must present movement in relation to music, position, and basic steps in a clear and enjoyable fashion.

Organization

A teacher of Country Western Dance should acquire an overall understanding of the theory behind Country Western Dances, sufficient knowledge of movement, rhythm and styling.

1. Be sure to know the dance correctly.

2. Basic Steps - Develop a good vocabulary of basic steps and analyze them.

3. Formations - Understand the different formations in which dances are performed. Sometimes formations are helpful in the execution of certain dances.

4. Positions - Understand the different positions used in dances. Certain positions are helpful in executing the movements.

5. Background - Study the background of each dance: choreographer, region, particular occasion for the dance and styling.

6. Rhythm - Understand the rhythmic structure of the dance: introduction, parts, interludes and transitions.

7. Music - Use recording which is intended for the dance.

8. Sound system - If possible, use a machine with variable speed control. It is easier for teaching purposes to slow down the tempo.

9. Microphone - be sure to use a wireless microphone.

10. Space - A wooden floor is preferred. Some dance movements are strenuous. A wooden floor has more flexibility and is less stressful to the body.

11. Footwear - Recommend footwear suitable for dancing. Boots are preferred. If this is not possible, strive for low-heeled, comfortable shoes. Shy away from loose footwear which could cause injury.

Planning

A good teacher will plan a lesson well in advance, taking into account the age group, sexes, abilities and knowledge already possessed by the group. Always progress from easy dances to the more complex. Begin with non-partner dances to create a social feeling, and most importantly, prepare more material than needed for the teaching session to add flexibility if needed.

1. Lesson Plan - Write out the objectives you wish to accomplish day by day, which Basic Steps need to be taught, rhythmic structures and dances, and the order by which they will be taught.

2. Basic Steps - Analyze the Basic Steps and remember to break them down into the basic locomotor or non-locomotor movements. Then combine them to form the Basic Steps in the dance. Be prepared to teach each Basic Step in a different way in order to reach all dancers in the group. Teach simple dances that have one or two Basic Steps. It's more fun that way.

3. Placement of Teacher - The placement of the teacher is essential. Most people learn through imitation. The teacher needs to be seen. In a circle, the teacher should be inside, off center, so the spacial directions are clear to the dancers. It is important for the teacher to move around the circle so that all dancers will get an equal chance to watch the steps performed in front of them.

    In a scatter (line) formation, the teacher should move and change walls quite often so all can see him/her.

    In couple dances, it is wise to teach the steps in a circle or scatter (line) formation (line)and then break into couples. The teacher should dance the man's part to show the lead.

    In a line dance, the teacher should lead the line until the dancers feel comfortable doing it on their own. Once the dancers know the dance, the teacher should step out so the dancers don't develop a dependency on the teacher.

4. Write Ups - Check the dance notation. If possible, look at all available notations and watch for variations. Some notations are filled with errors which could cause the dance to be misinterpreted.

5.   Rhythm - Analyze the music and develop a progressive break down which is clear to the dancers. Pay attention to accents in relation to movement. If needed, clap out the rhythm or practice stamping out accented beats.

6.   Cuing - Practice teaching the dance in a clear verbal manner cuing Basic Steps, phrases, transitions and repetitions in a rhythmical way. Be very precise about when to start (5, 6, 7, 8, or Ready, and...). Explain and cue introductions. If there is no introduction to the recording, use the first part as an introduction or let the melody play once through before beginning the dance.

Teaching Hints (Tips)

Each teacher has his or her own style of teaching. It is important to develop your own style rather than copy phrases and lines heard from another teacher. In other words, be yourself. Be spontaneous and aware at all times of the atmosphere created in the session. Keep it flowing and interesting. Remember, Country Western dance is fun!, share that feeling through your teaching.

1.   Atmosphere - Create a fun and relaxed atmosphere. Name the dance to be taught, talk about the background of the dance and any anecdote that pertains to it. Perhaps demonstrate the dance. Add humor when appropriate throughout the lesson. Humor eases the tension and enhances the ability to learn.

2.   Awareness - Be aware at all times of the progress of the dancers. If a given basic step is not clear, offer an alternate break down of the same step. Use problem solving. Use imagery to clarify a basic step. If a dancer is having difficulty, do not call attention to it. Move nonchalantly around the group and end up in front of that dancer so that he or she can watch you again. Be complimentary at all times, especially when a movement is executed well. Encourage the dancers throughout the teaching session.

3.   Drill - Go through Basic Steps without any relation to formation or position. Let the dancers develop the ability to perform the step first.

4.   Walk Through - After teaching a sequence, do it again in the correct tempo without music, this is called a walk through. Next, try the movement to music.

5.   Transition - Pay careful attention to transitions between steps and different parts. Understanding of the transitions will result in a better performance of the dance.

6.   Teaching Progression -

      a.   Teach the steps.
      b.   Perform the steps rhythmically.
      c.   Add the formation and position.
      d.   Stylize the dance.

7.   Modification - Another word for modify is simplify, which means <u>simplify</u> a Basic Step don't change it. For example, a step-hop has two actions, a step followed by a hop. To simplify, take a slow step with the Right and hold rather than hop. This does not change the structure of the Basic Step.

8.   Results - Remember at all times that Country Western Dance is a recreational activity. Bear in mind that the correct atmosphere and movement development will create an enjoyable social activity for the dancers. If possible, teach the dance quickly so that positive results can be evident immediately.

9.   Creativity - Be creative when breaking down and analyzing difficult basic steps. Try not to develop a feeling that a certain step is too difficult. That will intimidate some dancers.

      For example, when teaching the polka, have the dancers gallop 8 times starting with Right to Right and gallop 8 times with Left to Left. Next, have them gallop 4 times with Right to Right and 4 times with Left to Left. Then gallop twice with Right to Right and twice with Left to Left. Finally, you will notice that they are doing the polka without the hop. By speeding up the tempo, the hop will be added on its own and the dancers have learned the polka effortlessly.

      The same type of creativity can be applied in teaching any other steps. All you have to do is analyze and break down each step to its simplest form of basic locomotor movement.

HISTORICAL BACKGROUND

Background

Country Western dance, as we know it today is more diversified social dance form than people perceive it to be. It has become a very popular social activity, allowing people from all walks of life to participate with a minimum of effort required to master the basic movements. Country Western dance offers a variety of dance styles to satisfy the needs of many, from individual dancers to couples and from recreational dancers to serious competitors.

Line dancing is the simplest form of Country Western dance. Dancers are arranged in a scatter formation, all facing the same direction and doing a series of steps. The dancers can either face one wall throughout the entire execution of the dance or can change to face other walls as the dance progresses. Sometimes line dances are arranged so that dancers stand in a circle formation, or in contra lines (two lines facing each other).

Couple dances are dances which have a given basic step and numerous variations, such as the Two-Step, Polka, East Coast Swing, Cha Cha, West Coast Swing and Waltz. They differ from ballroom dances by the manner in which they are executed and the variations used.

Partner dances are choreographed dances in which all the couples on the floor are doing the same step at the same time. Variations are executed, but dancers move around the dance floor in unison.

Mixers are dances designed to be done with a partner. At the completion of each dance repetition, dancers end up with a new partner.

Competition is available for those who want to move beyond dance as recreation. As in ballroom competition, it is intended to be judged and certain rules are to be followed. It is no longer a recreational dance.

History

Country Western dance has exploded across the country as a social dance form. It is believed that the movie "Urban Cowboy" had a tremendous effect on popularizing this form of dance. Up to this point, Country Western dancing was found only in certain areas of the country with only a few dances in the repertoire.

Historically, the only true American dance was done by the Native Americans. As the early European settlers arrived in this country, they brought with them the dances of their homelands. As time passed, new dances and dance types were created, influenced by the traditional folk dances brought over from Europe. As a result, four types of dances emerged in early America: square dances, long-ways sets (contra), round dances and circle dances.

Square dancing is a contemporary development of the European quadrilles. A quadrille consisted of four couples. A basic quadrille had a sequence of a given number of parts and a chorus which was repeated between dance parts. Side couples repeated the movement of the head couples. Square dance is organized in much the same manner. The main difference lying in the cuing of the dance. Quadrilles were cued by sequences, square dance callers cue each movement.

Long-ways sets came from the English. Contra dances are long-ways sets of couples divided into active and inactive couples. The contra had a progression to it. Active couples would dance toward the bottom of the contra and upon reaching become inactive. Conversely, inactive couples would dance toward the top of the contra to become active. The American contra line dance (long-ways set) has only two lines facing each other with no progression.

Round dances are a pure American innovation. They consist of couple dances utilizing ballroom steps in an arranged sequence. Round dances have a caller who, as in square dance, cues every movement.

Circle dances are composed of couples in a single circle. Throughout the dance couples change partners, making it a mixer dance.

On the most basic level, Country Western dance is a blend of everything American. It blends folk dancing (Kentucky running set, round dances) with African/American influences (jazz, tap, jitterbug and swing) and some white influences (jigs, schottische, hoe down and ballroom).

Just as America is a great melting pot, Country Western dance is a potpourri of dance forms and styles. It contains elements of dance from the world over.

In its early days, Country Western dance was done mainly in the southwest by cowboys and at times called "cowboy dances." According to dance historian, Lloyd Shaw, Country Western dances are based mainly on New England contras, quadrilles and Kentucky running sets. Later the waltz was introduced, a dance done to three beats of music, with a step to each beat. It has evolved into a dance with three steps to two counts. This was known as the early Texas Two-Step.

Today, the Two-Step is very similar to the Foxtrot. The Basic Step in the Foxtrot is the magic step, choreographed and introduced by Harry Fox. The rhythmic structure of the steps in the Foxtrot is slow-slow-quick-quick. This sequence of steps is done over six counts of music taking two long (slow) steps forward and two relaxed (quick) steps to the side. The Country Western Two-Step is done with the same rhythm, often beginning with two quick steps followed by two slow steps. The steps are all done moving forward in Line Of Dance (CCW) for the men, backward for the women. With changes in Country Western music to more of a "rock" format, four weight changes over six beats became easier than the original three weight changes to two beats of music.

Country Western dance today started in bars and "honky tonks." Before 1983, Country Western line dancing was not seen. Only couple dances, like the Two-Step, Cotton Eyed Joe were danced. As it grew in popularity Country Western dance had a shortage of knowledgeable instructors. Numerous variations to dances evolved and still exist. We find that Basic Steps, Positions and Formations are the same but given different names and/or descriptions. Country Western dance is subject to regional variations, and in many cases dances by the same title are done with completely different steps. Uniformity is one problem that Country Western dance has not been able to solve yet. It is becoming better with more national organizations working toward standardization.

Style

Style is the manner by which a given people move. In dance we find that each dance category has its own style which is well documented and practiced. Country Western dance, being an emerging and developing social dance form, does not yet have a clearly defined style of its own. As discussed earlier in the historical background, numerous influences have contributed to Country Western dance. The only stylistic forms of Country Western dance which are clear are the hand position in line dance -- thumbs in the belt, and the closed position in couple dancing which differs from ballroom -- man's right hand on woman's left shoulder and woman's right hand on top of man's right arm.

One of the things affecting style is the fact that most of the Country Western dance teachers, especially the nationally recognized teachers and choreographers, have had some kind of dance background prior to their involvement in Country Western dance. That background, whether in folk, clogging, ballroom, jazz, ballet, etc., brings with it a unique style which is passed on through that teacher.

Another factor which affects styling is competition dance. While competitors strive to develop amalgamations and a style that will enhance their performance, dancers pick up on these moves and try to emulate them, thus adding to the pool of variations which further prevent the development of a concise social dance style. Actually, to define style in Country Western dance is, at this time, difficult at best. In time, Country Western dance will establish a definite style of its own, as all other dance forms have done.

Dance Etiquette
and
Floor Plan

Dance Etiquette

On a dance floor, be it anywhere around the world, certain etiquette has to be followed. Couple or partner dances when progressing around the floor, always move in Line of Dance (CCW). There are two imaginary outside lanes on a dance floor. The outside lane is used for couples doing fast progressive dances. The inside lane is used for couples who do not progress as far. In Country Western dances the center of the floor is used for, line dancing and stationary couple dances.

Floor Plan

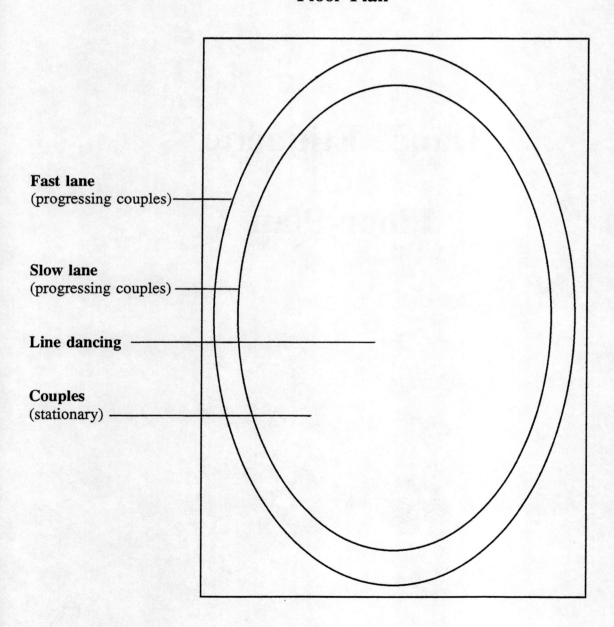

Fast lane
(progressing couples)

Slow lane
(progressing couples)

Line dancing

Couples
(stationary)

DANCE DESCRIPTIONS

All Shook Up

Scatter Formation

All Shook Up is a 48 count 4 Wall Line Dance. It was choreographed by Randy and Stephanie Krul. Suggested music: All Shook Up by Billy Joel (Honeymoon in Vegas Soundtrack). Note: The dance was choreographed to fit this song. Omit the first 16 counts during the forth and sixth repetitions.

Step Description

R Grapevine w/ Toe Heel Struts
1	Touch R toe across L
2	Shift weight to R
3	Touch L toe to L
4	Shift weight to L
5	Touch R toe behind L
6	Shift weight to R
7	Touch L toe to L
8	Shift weight to L

R Kick Ball Changes
1	Kick R Fwd
&	Step R to R
2	Step L across R
3-8	Repeat CTS. 1-2 three more times.

Side Toe Touches, Cross Steps
1	Touch R toe to R
2	Step R across L
3	Touch L toe to L
4	Step L across R
5-8	Repeat counts 1-4

All Shook Up Continued......

Step Description

R Kicks, R Bkwd Shuffle
1   Kick R Fwd
2   Kick R to R
3   Step R Bkwd
&   Step L beside R
4   Step R Bkwd

L Kicks, L Shuffle Bkwd
1   Kick L Fwd
2   Kick L to L
3   Step L Bkwd
&   Step R beside L
4   Step L Bkwd

Heel & Toe Swivels to R
1   Swivel heels to R, moving to R
2   Swivel toes to R, moving to R
3   Swivel heels to R, moving to R
4   Swivel toes to center

L Break Turns
1   Step R Fwd
2   Pivot on R turning a 1/2 turn to L (CCW), shift weight to L
3-4   Repeat CTS. 1-2

1/4 Turn, Pelvic Thrust
&   Step R to R while turning a 1/4 turn to R (CW)
1   Step L beside R
2   Hold
3   Pelvic thrust Fwd (could use arms in a pulling motion)
4   Hold

Hip & Body Shake
1-4   Shake body for 4 counts. (Use your imagination)

Arizona Strut

Scatter Formation

Arizona Strut is a 40 count 4 Wall Line Dance. The choreographer is unknown to author. Suggested music: Whiskey Ain't Working Anymore by Travis Tritt, Tryin' To Get To New Orleans by The Tractors, Swing The Mood by Jive Bunny & The Mastermixers.

Step Description

R Diag Fwd Step, Slide, R Diag Fwd Step, Touch
1   Step R diag Fwd to R
2   Slide L beside R
3   Step R diag Fwd to R
4   Touch L beside R

L Diag Fwd Step, Slide, L Diag Fwd Step, Touch
1   Step L diag Fwd to L
2   Slide R beside L
3   Step L diag Fwd to L
4   Touch R beside R

R Diag Bkwd Step, Slide, R Diag Bkwd Step, Touch
1   Step R diag Bkwd to R
2   Slide L beside R
3   Step R diag Bkwd to R
4   Touch L beside R

L Diag Bkwd Step, Slide, L Diag Bkwd Step, Touch
1   Step L diag Bkwd to L
2   Slide R beside L
3   Step L diag Bkwd to L
4   Step R beside L

Arizona Strut Continued.....

Step Description

Step, Stomp Up, Step, Stomp Up
1   Step L to L
2   Stomp Up R beside L
3   Step R to R
4   Stomp Up L beside R

L Vine, Stomp Up
1   Step L to L
2   Step R behind L
3   Step L to L
4   Stomp Up R beside L

R Vine, Stomp Up
1   Step R to R
2   Step L behind R
3   Step R to R
4   Stomp Up L beside R

Fwd Steps, Scuffs
1   Step L Fwd
2   Scuff R Fwd, clap hands
3   Step R Fwd
4   Scuff L Fwd, clap hands
5-8   Repeat CTS. 1-4

L Bkwd Vine, 1/4 Turn, Touch
1   Step L Bkwd
2   Step R Bkwd
3   Step L Bkwd while turning a 1/4 turn to L (CCW)
4   Touch R beside L

Arkansas Strut

(Country Boy)

Scatter Formation

Arkansas Strut is a 32 count 4 Wall Line Dance. The choreographer is unknown to author. Suggested music: Wher'm I Gonna Live by Billy Ray Cyrus, Stray Cat Strut by Stray Cats.

Step Description

Fwd Heel Touches, Steps
1	Touch R heel Fwd
2	Step R beside L
3	Touch L heel Fwd
4	Step L beside R
5-8	Repeat CTS. 1-4

Heel & Toe Touches
1-2	Touch R heel Fwd twice
3-4	Touch R toe Bkwd twice
5	Touch R heel Fwd
6	Touch R toe Bkwd
7-8	Repeat CTS. 5-6

Fwd Heel & Toe Struts → Basic E
1	Touch R heel Fwd
2	Step onto R
3	Touch L heel Fwd
4	Step onto L
5-8	Repeat CTS. 1-4

62

Arkansas Strut Continued.....

Step Description

Left Jazz Box, 1/4 Turn -BS

1   Step R across L
2   Step L Bkwd
3   Step R to R while turning a 1/4 turn to R (CW)
4   Step L beside R

Left Jazz Box -BS

1   Step R across L
2   Step L Bkwd
3   Step R to R
4   Step L beside R

Back in Texas

Scatter Formation

Back In Texas is a 32 count 2 Wall Line Dance. The dance was choreographed by Vicky Vance Johnson and Kevin Johnson. Suggested music: Dust On The Bottle by David Lee Murphy, No News by Lonestar.

Step Description

R Cross, Side, R Cross, Touch
1   Step R across L, turning body to L
2   Step L to L, turning body to face front
3   Step R across L, turning body to L
4   Touch L to L, turning body to face front

L Cross, Side, L Cross, Touch
1   Step L across R, turning body to R
2   Step R to R, turning body to face front
3   Step L across R, turning body to R
4   Touch R to R, turning body to face front

Stomp, R Fan
1   Stomp R Fwd
&   Turn R toes to R
2   Turn R toes to center

Stomp, L Fan
1   Stomp L Fwd
&   Turn L toes to L
2   Turn L toes to center

Back in Texas Continued.....

Step Description

R Charleston
1   Step R Fwd
2   Kick L Fwd
3   Step L Bkwd
4   Touch R Bkwd

L Break Turns
1   Step R Fwd
2   Pivot on R while turning a 1/2 turn to L (CCW), shift weight to L
3-4   Repeat CTS. 1-2

Cross, Unwind - 1/2 Turn, Fwd Jumps
1   Step R across L
2   Unwind (pivot on toes) a 1/2 turn to L (CCW)
3-4   Jump Fwd twice

Diag. Fwd Shuffles with Hip Bumps
1   Step R diag Fwd to R, bump R hip Fwd
&   Step L beside R, bump L hip Bkwd
2   Step R diag Fwd to R, bump R hip Fwd
3   Step L diag Fwd to L, bump L hip Fwd
&   Step R beside L, bump R hip Bkwd
4   Step L diag Fwd to L, bump L hip Fwd

Fwd Shuffles
1   Step R Fwd
&   Step L beside R
2   Step R Fwd
3   Step L Fwd
&   Step R beside L
4   Step L Fwd

The Barn Dance

Closed Position

The Barn Dance is a 32 count Couple Mixer Dance. Its a traditional dance. The choreographer is unknown. Partners are in Closed Position, Man's Back to center, Woman faces center. Suggested music: Wild, Wild, West by The Escape Club.

Step Description

Note: Man's steps described, Woman does opposite footwork.

L Side Step, Together, L Side Step, Touch
1   Step L to L
2   Step R beside L
3   Step L to L
4   Touch R beside L

R Side Step, Together, R Side Step, Touch
1   Step R to R
2   Step L beside R
3   Step R to R
4   Touch L beside R

L Side Step, Together, L Side Step, Touch, Turn Under
Man:
1   Step L to L while lifting L hand and turning the Woman under his L arm
2   Step R beside L
3   Step L to L
4   Touch R beside L

The Barn Dance Continued.....

Step Description

Woman:

1-3	Turn a full turn to R (CW), under Man's L arm with 3 steps: R, L, R
4	Touch L beside R

R Side Step, Together, R Side Step, Touch, 3/4 Turn Under
Man:

1	Step R to R while turning the Woman under his L arm
2	Step L beside R
3	Step R to R
4	Touch L beside R, while turning a 1/4 turn to L (CCW)

Woman:

1-3	Turn a 3/4 turn to L (CCW), under Man's L arm with 3 steps: L, R, L
4	Touch L beside R

Note: Partners end, side by side, both facing LOD (CCW), holding inside hands: Man's R and Woman's L.

Fwd Steps, Hitches

1	Step L Fwd
2	Hitch R
3	Step R Fwd
4	Hitch L
5-8	Repeat CTS. 1-4.

L Vine, Clap

1	Step L to L
2	Step R behind L
3	Step L to L
4	Touch R beside L, clap hands

R Vine, Clap

1	Step R to R
2	Step L behind R
3	Step R to R
4	Touch L beside R, clap hands

Note: End with a new partner, Man moves Fwd (CCW) to a new Woman, Woman moves Fwd (CW) to a new Man.

Bar Stools

Scatter Formation

Bar Stools is a 28 count 4 Wall Line Dance. The choreographer is unknown to the author. Suggested Music: Tall, Tall Trees by Alan Jackson, Any way The Wind Blows by Brother Phelps.

Step Description

R Hook
1	Touch R heel Fwd
2	Hook R heel across L
3	Touch R heel Fwd
4	Step R beside L

Butterfly (Heel Splits), Claps
1	Turn heels out
2	Turn heels in
3-4	Clap hands twice

Side Steps, Touches
1	Step R to R
2	Touch L beside R
3	Step L to L
4	Touch R beside L

R Vine, Touch
1	Step R to R
2	Step L behind R
3	Step R to R
4	Touch L beside R

Bar Stools Continued.....

Step Description

Side Steps, Touches
1   Step L to L
2   Touch R beside L
3   Step R to R
4   Touch L beside R

L Vine, Scuff, 1/4 Turn
1   Step L to L
2   Step R behind L
3   Step L to L while turning a 1/4 turn to L (CCW)
4   Scuff R Fwd

Fwd Step, Fwd Slide (Lock), Fwd Step, Stomp
1   Step R Fwd
2   Slide (lock) L Fwd behind R
3   Step R Fwd
4   Stomp L beside R

Bartender Stomp

(a.k.a. Mu Mu)

Scatter Formation

Bartender Stomp is a 24 count 4 Wall Line Dance. The Choreographer is unknown to author. Suggested music: Homesick by: Travis Tritt.

Step Description

R Vine, Touch -85
1	Step R to R
2	Step L behind R
3	Step R to R
4	Touch L beside R

L Vine, Touch -85
1	Step L to L
2	Step R behind L
3	Step L to L
4	Touch R beside L

R Bkwd Vine, Touch 85
1-3	Take 3 steps Bkwd: R, L, R
4	Touch L beside R

Step, Stomp Up, Step, Stomp Up
1	Step L Fwd
2	Stomp Up R beside L
3	Step R Bkwd
4	Stomp Up L beside R

Bartender Stomp Continued.....

Step Description

Step, Stomp Up, Hold, Syncopated Stomp Ups
  1   Step L Fwd
  2   Stomp Up R beside L
  3   Hold
&4   Stomp Up R beside L twice

Step, Touch, Step, Scuff, 1/4 Turn
  1   Step R Bkwd
  2   Touch L beside R
  3   Step L Fwd
  4   Scuff R while turning a 1/4 turn to L (CCW)

Boot Scootin' Boogie

Scatter Formation

This version of Boot Scootin' Boogie is a 17 count 4 Wall Line Dance. The Choreographer is Unknown to author. Suggested music: Boot Scootin' Boogie by Brooks and Dunn.

Step Description

R Fwd Scoots, Hitch
1-2   Scoot on R Fwd twice (L is hitched)

Step, Slide, Step, Stomp Up
1   Step L Fwd
2   Slide R Fwd beside L
3   Step L Fwd
4   Stomp Up R beside L

R Bkwd Vine, Scoot, Hitch
1-3   Take 3 steps Bkwd: R, L, R
4   Scoot R in place (L is hitched)

L Vine, Scoot, Hitch
1   Step L to L
2   Step R behind L
3   Step L to L
4   Scoot L in place (R is hitched)

R Vine, 1/4 Turn
1   Step R to R
2   Step L behind R
3   Step R to R while turning a 1/4 turn to R (CW)

Canadian Stomp

Scatter Formation

Canadian Stomp is a 36 count 4 Wall Line Dance. The Choreographer is Unknown to author. Suggested music: Any Man Of Mine by Shania Twain.

Step Description

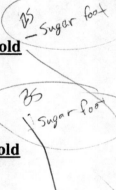

R Toe & Heel Touches, Stomp, Hold
1	Touch R toe beside L
2	Touch R heel beside L
3	Stomp R Fwd
4	Hold

BS — Sugar foot

L Toe & Heel Touches, Stomp, Hold
1	Touch L toe beside R
2	Touch L heel beside R
3	Stomp L Fwd
4	Hold

BS Sugar foot

Repeat the first 8 CTS.

Bkwd Step, Hold, Bkwd Step, Hold
1	Step R Bkwd
2	Hold
3	Step L Bkwd
4	Hold

Bkwd Steps, Stomp Up, Hold
1-2	Take 2 steps Bkwd: R, L
3	Stomp Up R beside L
4	Hold

74

Canadian Stomp Continued......

Step Description

Side Step, Side Slide, Side Step, Touch
1   Step R to R
2   Slide L beside R
3   Step R to R
4   Touch L beside R

L Vine, Scuff, 1/4 Turn
1   Step L to L
2   Step R behind L
3   Step L to L
4   Scuff R Fwd while turning a 1/4 turn to L (CCW)

L Jazz Box
1   Step R across L
2   Step L Bkwd
3   Step R to R
4   Step L beside

Caribbean Cowboy

Scatter Formation

Caribbean Cowboy is a 64 count 2 Wall Line Dance. It was choreographed by Ed Henry. Suggested music: Hot, Hot, Hot by Buster Poindexter.

Step Description

R Side Steps, Together, Step, Touch, Clap (Caribbean Walk)
1	Step R to R
2	Step L beside R
3-6	Repeat CTS. 1-2 twice more
7	Step R to R
8	Touch L beside R, clap hands

L Side Steps, Together, Step, Touch, Clap (Caribbean Walk)
1	Step L to L
2	Step R beside L
3-6	Repeat CTS. 1-2 twice more
7	Step L to L
8	Touch R beside L, clap hands

R Side Step, Hold, L Slide, Clap, Shimmy
1	Step R to R (could shimmy)
2	Hold
3	Step L beside R (could shimmy)
4	Clap hands
5-6	Repeat CTS. 1-2
7	Touch L beside R
8	Clap hands

Caribbean Cowboy Continued....

Step Description

L Side Step, Hold, Slide, Clap, Shimmy
1	Step L to L (could shimmy)
2	Hold
3	Step R beside L (could shimmy)
4	Clap hands
5-6	Repeat CTS. 1-2
7	Touch R beside L
8	Clap hands

L Military Turns (1/4 Turns)
1	Turn a 1/4 turn to L (CCW) by lifting the L toe and R heel
2	Step R beside L
3-8	Repeat CTS. 1-2, 3 more times. complete a full turn

R Military Turns (1/4 Turns)
1	Turn a 1/4 turn to R (CW) by lifting the R toe and L heel
2	Step L beside R
3-8	Repeat CTS. 1-2, 3 more times. complete a full turn

R Bkwd Rock, Cha Cha
1	Rock R Bkwd
2	Rock L Fwd
3	Step R beside L
&	Step L in place beside R
4	Step R in place beside L

L Bkwd Rock, Cha Cha
1	Rock L Bkwd
2	Rock R Fwd
3	Step L beside R
&	Step R in place beside L
4	Step L in place beside R

Kick, Cross, Unwinding 1/2 Turn, Squat
1	Kick R Fwd
2	Step R across L
3	Unwind, turn a 1/2 turn to L (CCW)
4	Bend knees (squat position)

Hip Thrusts
1	Thrust R hip to R
2	Thrust L hip to L
3-4	Repeat CTS. 1-2

Cherokee Kick

Circle Formation

Cherokee Kick is a 34 count Circle Dance. Formation: Individuals in a single circle, facing in. The choreographer is unknown to author. Suggested music: Fishin' In The Dark by the Nitty Gritty Dirt Band, Copperhead Road by Steve Earle.

Step Description

Heel Swivels, Heel & Toe Touches
1   Swivel heels to R
2   Swivel heels to center
3   Swivel heels to L
4   Swivel heels to center
5   Touch R heel Fwd
6   Touch R toe Bkwd

Charleston, Fwd Step, Kick
1   Step R Fwd
2   Kick L Fwd
3   Step L Bkwd
4   Touch R Bkwd
5   Step R Fwd
6   Kick L Fwd

Side Steps & Touches
1   Step L to L
2   Touch R beside L and clap hands
3   Step R to R
4   Touch L beside R and clap hands
5   Step L to L
6   Touch R beside L and clap hands

Cherokee Kick Continued.....

Step Description

Side Behind, Step-Hops, 1 Turn and a 1/4
1   Step R to R
2   Step L behind R
3-8   3 Step-hops; R, L, R, while turning a turn and a 1/4 to R (CW), Progressing on the line of the circle (CCW)

Fwd Steps, Hitch, Fwd Scoots, Step, 1/4 Turn, Stomp
1   Step L Fwd
2   Step R Fwd
3-4   Scoot R Fwd twice, while L is hitched
5   Step L Fwd
6   Step R Fwd
7   Step L in place while turning a 1/4 turn to L (CCW), (face center)
8   Stomp R beside L

Cotton Eyed Joe
(Contra)

Contra Line

This version of Cotton Eyed Joe is a 48 count 2 Wall Contra Line Dance. The choreographer is unknown to author. Suggested music: Cotton Eyed Joe by Rednex.

Dance Description

Hook L, Kick, L Triple Step
1   Hook L across R
2   Kick L Fwd
3   Step L in place
&   Step R beside L
4   Step L in place

Hook R, Kick, R Triple Step
1   Hook R across L
2   Kick R Fwd
3   Step R in place
&   Step L beside R
4   Step R in place

Fwd Step, Slide, Fwd Step, Kick, Clap
1   Step L Fwd
2   Slide R beside L
3   Step L Fwd
4   Kick R Fwd and clap hands with dancer in front of you.

Bkwd Steps (Reels), L Triple Step
1   Step R Bkwd behind L (reel)
2   Step L Bkwd behind R (reel)
3   Step R in place
&   Step L beside R
4   Step R in place

Cotton Eyed Joe (Contra) Continued...........

Step Description

L Grapevine, Heel & Toe Touches, Brush, Stomp
1	Step L across R
2	Step R to R
3	Step L behind R
4	Step R to R
5	Touch L heel Fwd
6	Touch L toe Bkwd
7	Brush L Fwd
8	Stomp L beside R

R Grapevine, Heel & Toe Touches, Brush, Stomp
1	Step R across L
2	Step L to L
3	Step R behind L
4	Step L to L
5	Touch R heel Fwd
6	Touch R toe Bkwd
7	Brush R Fwd
8	Stomp R beside L

Hip Bumps, 1/2 Turn
1-2	Step L Fwd while turning a 1/4 turn to R (CW), bump L hip twice Fwd, toward opposite dancer
3-4	Bump R hip Bkwd twice, away from opposite dancer
5-6	Step L while turning a 1/2 turn to L (CCW), bump L hip Bkwd twice, away from opposite dancer
7-8	Bump R hip Fwd twice, toward opposite dancer

Fwd Shuffles, 1 and a 1/2 Turns
1	Step L Fwd, while turning a 1/4 turn to R (CW).
&	Step R beside L
2	Step L Fwd

Note: During the next 3 shuffles turn L (CCW) a turn and a 1/2 changing places with the opposite dancer.

3	Step R Fwd
&	Step L beside R
4	Step R Fwd
5-8	Repeat CTS. 1-4 (while completing the turn, end on the opposite line)

Cotton Eyed Joe
(Couple)

Varsouvienne Position

This version of Cotton Eyed Joe is a 32 count Couple Dance. It is one of the oldest Couple Novelty Dances done in the country. The formation is couples in Side by Side Position, Man on the L, Woman on the R, with hands joined in Sweetheart (Varsovienne), position. The choreographer is unknown to author. Suggested music: Cotton Eyed Joe, Any version.

Step Description

Hook L, Kick, L Bkwd Shuffle
1	Hook L across R
2	Kick L Fwd
3	Step L Bkwd
&	Step R Bkwd beside L
4	Step L Bkwd

Hook R, Kick, R Bkwd Shuffle
1	Hook R across L
2	Kick R Fwd
3	Step R Bkwd
&	Step L Bkwd beside R
4	Step R Bkwd

Repeat The First 8 CTS.

Fwd Shuffles
1	Step L Fwd
&	Step R beside L
2	Step L Fwd
3	Step R Fwd
&	Step L beside R
4	Step R Fwd

Cotton Eyed Joe (Couple) Continued.....

Step Description

Fwd Shuffles Continued....

5-16   Repeat CTS. 1-4, 3 more times

Note: During the 8 Shuffle step Fwd, the Man could turn the Woman under his R arm as many turn as he wishes. Normally the Woman would turn 1 full turn (CW) with 2 Shuffle steps.

Cowboy Boogie

Scatter Formation

Cowboy Boogie is a 24 count 4 Wall Line Dance. The choreographer is unknown to author. Suggested music: Elvira by The Oakridge Boys, Wherever You Go by Clint Black, Honky Tonk Walkin' by The Kentucky Headhunters, Dancin' Shoes by Ronnie McDowell.

Step Description

R Vine, Scuff
1	Step R to R
2	Step L behind R
3	Step R to R
4	Scuff L Fwd

L Vine, Scuff
1	Step L to L
2	Step R behind L
3	Step L to L
4	Scuff R Fwd

Fwd Steps, Scuffs
1	Step R Fwd
2	Scuff L Fwd
3	Step L Fwd
4	Scuff R Fwd

R Bkwd Vine, Hitch
1-3	Take 3 steps Bkwd: R, L, R
4	Hitch L

Double Hip Bumps
1-2	Step L diag Fwd to L, bump L hip Fwd twice
3-4	Bump R hip diag Bkwd twice

Cowboy Boogie Continued.....

Step Description

Single Hip Bumps, Scuff, 1/4 Turn

1   Bump L hip diag Fwd
2   Bump R hip diag Bkwd
3   Bump L hip diag Fwd
4   Scuff R Fwd while turning a 1/4 turn to L (CCW)

Cowboy Cha Cha

Scatter Formation

Cowboy Cha Cha is a 20 count 4 Wall Line Dance. The Choreographer is unknown to author. Suggested music: Neon Moon by Brooks and Dunn, Rock 'N Roll Angel by The Kentucky Headhunters.

Step Description

L Fwd Rock, Cha-Cha
1	Rock L Fwd
2	Rock R Bkwd
3	Step L Bkwd
&	Step R Bkwd beside L
4	Step L Bkwd

R Bkwd Rock
1	Rock R Bkwd
2	Rock L Fwd

1/4 Turn, R Side Cha Cha, L Bkwd Diag Rock
1	Step R to R, while turning a 1/4 turn to L (CCW)
&	Step L beside R
2	Step R to R
3	Rock L Diag behind R
4	Rock R Fwd

L Side Cha Cha, R Bkwd Diag Rock
1	Step L to L
&	Step R beside L
2	Step L to L
3	Rock R Diag behind L
4	Rock L Fwd

No single action!

86

Cowboy Cha Cha Continued.....

Step Description

R Side Cha Cha
1	Step R to R
&	Step L beside R
2	Step R to R

R Break Turns
1	Step L Fwd
2	Pivot on L while turning a 1/2 turn to R (CW), shift weight to R
3-4	Repeat CTS. 1-2

Cowboy Hip Hop

Scatter Formation

Cowboy Hip Hop is a 32 count 1 Wall Line Dance. The choreographers are Vicky Vance Johnson and Kevin Johnson. Suggested music: Yippy Ti Yi Yo by Ronnie McDowell.

Step Description

Step Hops (Chugs)
1	Step R in Pl.
&	Hop (Chug) R Bkwd while hitching L
2	Step L in place
&	Hop (Chug) L Bkwd while hitching R
3-4	Repeat CTS. 1-2

Hip Circles
1-2	Step R Fwd while circling hips one full turn CW
3-4	Circle hips one full turn CCW

Bkwd Rocking Chair
1	Rock R Bkwd
2	Rock L Fwd
3	Rock R Fwd
4	Rock L Bkwd

Bkwd Rocking Chair (Double Time)
1	Leap R Bkwd while L kicks Fwd
&	Leap L in place while R kicks Bkwd
2	Leap Fwd onto R while L kicks Bkwd
&	Leap L in place while R kicks Fwd
3	Leap R Bkwd while L kicks Fwd
&	Leap L in place while R kicks Bkwd
4	Leap Fwd onto R while L kicks Bkwd
&	Touch L beside R

Cowboy Hip Hop Continued.....

Step Description

L Vine, Stomp Up, Clap
1   Step L to L
2   Step R behind L
3   Step L to L
4   Stomp Up R beside L while clapping hands

Lunge, Slide, Steps
1   Lunge R to R
2   Slide L beside R
3-4   Take 2 steps in place: R, L

Jumping Jacks, 1/2 turn
1   Jump with feet apart
&   Jump with feet together
2   Jump with feet apart
&   Jump with feet together while turning a 1/2 turn to L (CCW)
3   Jump with feet apart
&   Jump with feet together
4   Jump with feet apart
&   Shift weight to L

Ball Changes, 1/8 Turn
1   Step on ball of R diag Fwd to R, bump R hip to R
&   Step on L in place while turning an 1/8 turn to L
2   Step on ball of R diag Fwd to R, bump R hip to R
&   Step on L in place while turning an 1/8 turn to L
3   Step on ball of R diag Fwd to R, bump R hip to R
&   Step on L in place while turning an 1/8 turn to L
4   Step on ball of R diag Fwd to R, bump R hip to R
&   Step on L in place while turning an 1/8 turn to L
     Note: Turn a 1/2 turn to L during the last 4 CTS. to end facing original wall.

Cowgirls' Twist

Scatter Formation

Cowgirl's Twist is a 32 count 4 Wall Line Dance. The choreographer is Bill Bader. Suggested music: What The Cowgirls Do by Vince Gill, Rock 'N' Roll Angel by The Kentucky Headhunters.

Step Description

Fwd Heel & Toe Struts
1   Touch R heel Fwd
2   Step onto R
3   Touch L heel Fwd
4   Step onto L
5-8 Repeat CTS. 1-4

Bkwd Steps
1-3 Take 3 steps Bkwd: R, L, R
4   Step L beside R

Heel & Toe Swivels to L, Hold, Clap
1   Swivel heels to L
2   Swivel toes to L, traveling to L
3   Swivel heels to L, traveling to L
4   Hold and clap hands

Heel & Toe Swivels to R, Hold, Clap
1   Swivel heels to R
2   Swivel toes to R, traveling to R
3   Swivel heels to R, traveling to R
4   Hold and clap hands

Heel Swivel To L, Hold, Clap
1   Swivel heels to L
2   Hold and clap hands

Cowgirls' Twist Continued......

Step Description

Heel Swivel To R, Hold, Clap
1   Swivel heels to R
2   Hold and clap hands

Heel Swivels, Hold, Clap
1   Swivel heels to L
2   Swivel heels to R
3   Swivel heels to Center
4   Hold and clap hands

Step, Hold, 1/4 Turn, Hold
1   Step R Fwd hold, lean shoulders Fwd
2   Hold
3   Step L while turning a 1/4 turn to L (CCW)
4   Hold

Cruisin'

Scatter Formation

Cruisin' is a 32 count 1 Wall Line Dance. The choreographer is Dean Rhonemus. Suggested music: Cruisin' by The Beach Boys, Wanda by Forester Sisters.

Step Description

basic   basic

L Diag Fwd Rock / L Cha Cha
1	Rock L diag Fwd across R
2	Rock R Bkwd
3-4	Cha Cha step in place: L, R, L

R Diag Fwd Rock / R Cha Cha
1	Rock R diag Fwd across L
2	Rock L Bkwd
3-4	Cha Cha step in place: R, L, R

L Fwd Rock / L Cha Cha
1	Rock L Fwd
2	Rock R Bkwd
3-4	Cha Cha step in place: L, R, L

R Bkwd Rock / R Cha Cha
1	Rock R Bkwd
2	Rock L Fwd
3-4	Cha Cha step in place: R, L, R

R Break Turns
1	Step L Fwd
2	Pivot on L while turning a 1/2 turn to R (CW), shift weight to R
3-4	Repeat CTS. 1-2

Cruisin' Continued.....

Step Description

L Vine, L Turn, R Vine, R Turn

Note: During the next 12 CTS. you are going to execute a figure 8

1   Step L to L

2   Step R behind L

3   Step L to L

4-5   Turn a full turn to L (CCW) as follows: Step R across L while turning L (CCW), Step L Fwd while continuing the turn to L (CCW)

6   Step R to R, completing the full turn. end facing original wall.

7   Step L behind R

8   Step R to R

9-11 Turn a full turn to R (CW) as follows: Step L across R while turning R, (CW), Step R Fwd, still turning R (CW), Step L Fwd, while completing the turn (CW)

12   Step R beside L (face original wall)

Dancin' Feet

Scatter Formation

Dancin' Feet is a 40 count 2 Wall Line Dance. The Choreographer is Susan Brooks. Suggested music: "Music That You Can Dance To" by Retro Rock Dance Hits, Wipe Out by The Beach Boys, Heaven Bound (I'm Ready) by Shenandoah.

Step Description

R Front Sailor Step
1   Step R across L
&   Step L to L
2   Step R to R

L Sailor Step
1   Step L behind R
&   Step R to R
2   Step L to L

R Cross, Side Step
1   Step R across L
2   Step L to L

R Sailor Step
1   Step R behind L
&   Step left to L
2   Step R to R

L Front Sailor Step
1   Step L across R
&   Step R to R
2   Step L to L

Dancin' Feet Continued......

Step Description

R Sailor Step
1	Step R behind L
&	Step L to L
2	Step R to R

L Cross, Side Step
1	Step L across R
2	Step R to R

L Sailor Step
1	Step L behind R
&	Step R to R
2	Step L to L

R Vine(Double Time), 1/4 Turn
&	Step on ball of L to L
1	Step R across L
&	Step on ball of L to L
2	Step R behind L
&	Step on ball of L to L
3	Step R across L
4	Step L to L while turning a 1/4 turn to L (CCW)

Simplified Version - R Vine, 1/4 Turn
1	Step R across L
2	Step L to L
3	Step R behind L
4	Step L to L while turning a 1/4 turn to L (CCW)

L Break Turn, Fwd Shuffle
1	Step R Fwd
2	Pivot on R while turning a 1/2 turn to L (CCW), shift weight to L
3	Step R Fwd
&	Step L Fwd beside R
4	Step R Fwd

Dancing' Feet Continued......

Step Description

L Vine(Double Time), 1/4 Turn
&	Step on ball of R to R
1	Step L across R
&	Step on ball of R to R
2	Step L behind R
&	Step on ball of R to R
3	Step L across R
4	Step R to R while turning a 1/4 turn to R (CW)

Simplified Version - L Vine, 1/4 Turn
1	Step L across R
2	Step R to R
3	Step L behind R
4	Step R to R while turning a 1/4 turn to R (CW)

R Break Turn, Fwd Shuffle
1	Step L Fwd
2	Pivot on L while turning a 1/2 turn to R (CW), shift weight to R
3	Step L Fwd
&	Step R Fwd beside L
4	Step L Fwd

R Kick Ball Change With a 1/4 Turn
1	Kick R Fwd
&	Step back on ball of R
2	Step L in place while turning a 1/4 turn to L (CCW)
3&4	Repeat CTS. 1&2

Kick, Out Out, In In, Clap
1	Kick R Fwd
&	Step R to R
2	Step L to L (feet shoulders width apart)
&	Step R back to place
3	Step L back to place
4	Clap hands

Easy Walkin'

Scatter Formation

Easy Walkin' is a 20 count 4 Wall Line Dance. The Choreographer is Margaret McCabe. Suggested music: How Come You Go To Her by Suzy Bogguss, I Wonder by Roseanne Cash, I've Got A Lot to Learn by Brooks & Dunn.

Step Description

Fwd Steps, Touches
1	Step L Fwd
2	Touch R beside L
3	Step R Fwd
4	Touch L beside R

L Fwd Vine, Touch
1-3	Take 3 steps Fwd; L, R, L
4	Touch R beside L

Bkwd Step, Touch, Fwd Step, Touch
1	Step R back
2	Touch L beside R
3	Step L Fwd
4	Touch R Beside L

R Bkwd Vine (or 3 Step Turn), Touch
1-3	Take 3 steps Bkwd; R, L, R, (could turn a full turn Bkwd to R (CW)
4	Touch L beside R

Easy Walkin' Continued.....

Step Description

Side Step, Touch, Step, 1/4 Turn, Touch
1   Step L to L
2   Touch R beside L
3   Step R to Right while turning a 1/4 turn to R
4   Touch L Beside R

Electric Slide

Scatter Formation

Electric Slide is an 18 count 4 Wall Line Dance. The Choreographer is unknown to author. Suggested music: Shall We Dance by Grand Master Slice, I Feel Lucky by Mary Chapin Carpenter, Fast As You, by Dwight Yoakam.
Note: This version, done by Country Western dancers, is really a dance called The Freeze. The author feels that rather than confusing everybody, it's easier to just keep calling this dance The Electric Slide.

Step Description

R Vine, Touch
1	Step R to R
2	Step L behind R
3	Step R to R
4	Touch L beside R

L Vine, Touch
1	Step L to L
2	Step R behind L
3	Step L to L
4	Touch R beside L

R Bkwd Vine, Touch
1-3	Take 3 steps Bkwd: R, L, R
4	Touch L beside R

Electric Slide Continued.....

Step Description

Fwd Step, Touch, Bkwd Step, Touch
1   Step L Fwd
2   Touch R beside L
3   Step R Bkwd
4   Touch L beside R

Fwd Step, Scuff, 1/4 Turn
1   Step L Fwd
2   Scuff R while Turning a 1/4 Turn to L (CCW)

Foot Boogie

Contra Line

Foot Boogie is a 32 count 2 Wall Contra Line Dance. The choreographer is unknown to author. Suggested music: Kiss Me In The Car by John Berry, Baby Likes To Rock It by The Tractors.

Step Description

R Fans
1	Turn R toes to R
2	Turn R toes to center
3-4	Repeat CTS. 1-2

L Fans
1	Turn L toes to L
2	Turn L toes to center
3-4	Repeat CTS. 1-2

R Toe & Heel Swivels
1	Turn R toes to R
2	Turn R heel to R, feet are apart
3	Turn R heel to L
4	Turn R toes to center

L Toe & Heel Swivels
1	Turn L toes to L
2	Turn L heel to L, feet are apart
3	Turn L heel to R
4	Turn L toes to center

Foot Boogie Continued......

Step description

Toe & Heel Swivels
1   Turn both toes out
2   Turn both heels out, feet are apart
3   Turn both heels in
4   Turn both toes back to center

Fwd Step, Fwd Slide (Lock), Fwd Step, Hitch, Scoot
1   Step R Fwd
2   Slide L Fwd behind R
3   Step R Fwd
4   Scoot Fwd on the R while L is hitched

Fwd Step, Fwd Slide (Lock), Fwd Step, Hitch, 1/2 Turn
1   Step L Fwd
2   Slide R Fwd behind L
3   Step L Fwd
4   Turn a 1/2 turn to L (CCW) while R is hitched

Fwd Steps, Fwd Jump
1-3   Take 3 steps Fwd; L, R, L
4   Jump Fwd on both feet

Hooked on Country

Scatter Formation

Hooked On Country is a 32 count 4 Wall Line Dance . The choreographer is unknown to author. Suggested music: Hooked On Country by Atlanta Pops.

Step Description

Bkwd Shuffles
1	Step R Bkwd
&	Step L beside R
2	Step R Bkwd
3	Step L Bkwd
&	Step R beside L
4	Step L Bkwd

R Fwd Vine, Kick
1-3	Take 3 steps Fwd; R, L, R
4	Kick L Fwd

L Bkwd Vine, Syncopated Side Cross
1-3	Take 3 steps Bkwd; L, R, L
&	Step on ball of R foot to R
4	Step L across R

R Vine, Kick, Clap
1	Step R to R
2	Step L behind R
3	Step R to R
4	Kick L across R & clap hands

Hooked on Country Continued.....

Step Description

L Vine, Kick, Clap
1   Step L to L
2   Step R behind L
3   Step L to L
4   Kick R across L & clap hands

Side Step, Kick, Clap, Side Step, Kick, Clap
1   Step R to R
2   Kick L across R & clap hands
3   Step L to L
4   Kick R across L & clap hands

Heel & Toe Taps
1-2   Tap R heel Fwd twice
3-4   Tap R toes Bkwd twice

Fwd Step, 1/4 Turn, Stomp Up, Kick
1   Step R Fwd
2   Step L in place while turning a 1/4 turn to left (CCW)
3   Stomp Up R beside L
4   Kick R Fwd

Horsin' Around

Scatter Formation

Horsin' Around is a 32 count 4 Wall Line Dance. The Choreography was adapted by: Dick Matties & Geneva Owsley. Suggested music: Men by Forester Sisters, Trashy Women by Confederate Railroad.

Step Description

Heel Touches, Steps
1	Touch L heel Fwd
2	Step L beside R
3	Touch R Fwd
4	Step R beside L

L Heel Touches
1-2	Touch L heel twice, Diag Fwd to L
3-4	Touch L heel Fwd twice

L Heel & Toe Touches
1	Touch L toe Diag back to L
2	Touch L heel Fwd
3-4	Repeat CTS. 1-2

Pelvic Thrusts (Rein Pulls)
1	Step L Bkwd while touching R Fwd and arms extended Fwd waist high
2	Thrust pelvice Fwd as arms pull Bkwd
3	Push hips back as arms extend Fwd
4	Thrust pelvic Fwd as arms pull Bkwd

Horsin' Around Continued......

Step Description

1/4 Turn, R Vine, Hitch
1	Step R to R while turning a 1/4 turn to L
2	Step L behind R
3	Step R to R
4	Hitch L knee

L Vine, Hitch
1	Step L to L
2	Step R behind L
3	Step L to L
4	Hitch R knee

R Bkwd Vine
1-3	Take 3 steps Bkwd: R, L, R
4	Hitch L knee

Fwd Step, Fwd Slide, Fwd Step, Stomp
1	Step L Fwd
2	Slide R Fwd beside L
3	Step L Fwd
4	Stomp R beside L

Lazy Shuffle

Scatter Formation

Lazy Shuffle is a 32 count 4 Wall Line Dance. It was choreographed by: Judie Ishmael. Suggested music: I Wouldn't Wanna Be You by Reba McEntire, It's Love by Lari White.

Step Description

Fwd Shuffles
1	Step R Fwd
&	Step L beside R
2	Step R Fwd
3	Step L Fwd
&	Step R beside L
4	Step L Fwd

Fwd Rocks
1	Rock R Fwd
2	Rock L Bkwd
3-4	Repeat CTS. 1-2

Bkwd Shuffles
1	Step R Bkwd
&	Step L beside R
2	Step R Bkwd
3	Step L Bkwd
&	Step R beside L
4	Step L Bkwd

Lazy Shuffle Continued.....

Step Description

R Bkwd Rocks
1   Rock R Bkwd
2   Rock L Fwd
3-4   Repeat CTS. 1-2

R Step Behind, R Triple Step
1   Step R to R
2   Step L behind R
3   Step R beside L
&   Step L beside R
4   Step R beside L

L Step Behind, L Triple Step
1   Step L to L
2   Step R behind L
3   Step L beside R
&   Step R beside L
4   Step L beside R

Heel & Toe Touches
1-2   Touch R heel Fwd, twice
3-4   Touch R toe Bkwd twice

Heel & Toe Touches (Star), 1/4 Turn, Hook
1   Touch R heel Fwd
2   Touch R beside L
3   Touch R toe to R
4   Hook R across L while turning a 1/4 turn to L (CCW)

One Step Forward

One Step Forward is a 20 count 4 Wall Line Dance. The Choreographer is Unknown to author. Suggested music: One Step Forward by The Desert Rose Band.

Step Description

L Diag Fwd Step, Touch
1   Step L diag Fwd to L, lead with L shoulder
2   Touch R beside L

R Diag Bkwd Step, Slide, R Diag Bkwd Step, Slide, Touch
1   Step R diag Bkwd to R, lead with R shoulder
2   Slide L diag Bkwd beside R
3   Step R diag Bkwd to R
4   Touch L beside R

L Side Step, Slide, Step, Touch
1   Step L to L, face original wall
2   Slide R beside L
3   Step L to L
4   Touch R beside L

R Diag Fwd Step, Touch
1   Step R diag Fwd to R, lead with R shoulder
2   Touch L beside R

One Step Forward Continued.....

Step Description

L Diag Bkwd Step, Slide, Step, Touch
1   Step L Diag Bkwd to L, lead with L shoulder
2   Slide R Diag Bkwd beside L
3   Step L Diag Bkwd to L
4   Touch R beside L

Side Step, Slide, Step, Touch
1   Step R to R
2   Slide L beside R
3   Step R to R
4   Touch L beside R while turning a 1/4 turn to R (CW)

Rebel Strut

(a.k.a. Sixteen Step Polka)

Varsouvienne Position

Rebel Strut is a 24 count Couple dance. Dancers are side by side in Varsovienne Position, all facing LOD (CCW). The choreographer is unknown to author. Suggested music: Dance by Twister Alley

Step Description

R Hook
1   Touch R heel Fwd
2   Hook R across L
3   Touch R heel Fwd
4   Step R beside L

L Heel Touch, Step
1   Touch L toe Fwd
2   Step L beside R

R Toe Touch, Step
1   Touch R toe Bkwd
2   Step R beside L

L Heel Touch, Step, Stomp Ups
1   Touch L toe Fwd
2   Step L beside R
3-4   Stomp up R beside L twice

L Break Turns
(Drop R hands)
1   Step R Fwd
2   Pivot on R while turning a 1/2 turn to L (CCW), shift weight to L
3-4   Repeat CTS. 1-2

Rebel Strut Continued.....

Step Description

Fwd Shuffles
(Rejoin R hands)

1	Step R Fwd
&	Step L beside R
2	Step R Fwd
3	Step L Fwd
&	Step R beside L
4	Step L Fwd
5-8	Repeat CTS. 1-4

Redneck Girl

Scatter Formation

Redneck Girl is a 34 count 4 Wall Line Dance. The choreographer is unknown to author.
Suggested music: Redneck Girl by The Bellamy Brothers

Step Description

Fwd Heel Touches, Steps
1   Touch R heel Fwd
2   Step R beside L
3   Touch L heel Fwd
4   Step L beside R

Diag Bkwd Toe Touches, Steps
1   Touch R toe behind L
2   Step R beside L
3   Touch L toe behind R
4   Step L beside R

Heel & Toes Touches
1-2   Touch R heel Fwd twice
3-4   Touch R toe Bkwd twice

Scuff & Hook, 1/4 Turn
1   Scuff R heel Fwd
2   Hook R across L while turning a 1/4 turn to L (CCW)

Redneck Girl Continued.......

Step Description

R Vine, Touch
1   Step R to R
2   Step L behind R
3   Step R to R
4   Touch L beside R

L Vine, Touch
1   Step L to L
2   Step R behind L
3   Step L to L
4   Touch R beside L

R Bkwd Vine, Touch
1-3   Take 3 steps Bkwd: R, L, R
4   Touch L beside R

Fwd Step, Fwd Slide, Fwd Step, Stomp
1   Step L Fwd
2   Slide R Fwd beside L
3   Step L Fwd
4   Stomp R beside L

Butterflies (Heel Splits)
1   Turn heels out
2   Turn heels in
3-4   Repeat CTS. 1-2

Reggae Cowboy

Scatter Formation

Reggae Cowboy is an 18 count 4 Wall Line Dance . The choreographer is unknown to author. Suggested music: Get Into Reggae Cowboy by The Bellamy Brothers.

Step Description

Heel & Toe Touches, Steps
1	Touch R heel Fwd
2	Touch R toe beside L
3	Touch R heel Fwd
4	Step R beside L
5	Touch L heel Fwd
6	Touch L toe beside R
7	Touch L heel Fwd
8	Touch L toe beside R

Bkwd Step, Touch, Fwd Step, 1/4 Turn, Side Touch, Cross Step, Side Touch
1	Step L Bkwd
2	Touch R toe Bkwd
3	Step R Fwd
4	Touch L to L while pivoting a 1/4 turn to R (CW) on L
5	Step L across R
6	Touch R to R

Cross, Bkwd Step, Stomp Ups
1	Step R across L
2	Step Bkwd with L
3-4	Stomp Up R beside L twice

116

Reggae Cowboy II

Scatter Formation

Reggae Cowboy II is a 48 count 4 Wall Line Dance . It was choreographed by: Gene Schrivener. Suggested music: Get Into Reggae Cowboy by The Bellamy Brothers.

Step Description

Stomps, Claps
1	Stomp R Fwd
&2	Clap hands twice
3	Stomp L Fwd
&4	Clap hands twice
5-8	Repeat CTS. 1-4

R Bkwd Vine, Hitch
1-3	Take 3 steps Bkwd: R, L, R
4	Hitch L

L Bkwd Vine, Hitch
1-3	Take 3 steps Bkwd: L, R, L
4	Hitch R

R Vine, Touch
1	Step R to R
2	Step L behind R
3	Step R to R
4	Touch L beside R

Reggae Cowboy II Continued....

Step Description

L Vine, (3 Step Turn), Touch
1   Step L to L
2   Step R behind L
3   Step L to L
4   Touch R beside L
     Note: You could turn a full turn to L (CCW) instead of the L Vines

Repeat previous 8 Cts.

Fwd Shuffles, 1/8 Turn
1   Turn an 1/8 to R (face 1:30), Step R Fwd
&   Step L beside R
2   Step R Fwd
3   Step L Fwd
&   Step R beside L
4   Step L Fwd

Bkwd Shuffles, 1/4 Turn
1   Turn a 1/4 to R (face 4:30), Step R Bkwd
&   Step L beside R
2   Step R Bkwd
3   Step L Bkwd
&   Step R beside L
4   Step L Bkwd

Fwd Shuffles, 1/4 Turn
1   Turn a 1/4 to R (face 7:30), Step R Fwd
&   Step L beside R
2   Step R Fwd
3   Step L Fwd
&   Step R beside L
4   Step L Fwd

Bkwd Shuffles, 1/8 Turn
1   Turn a 1/8 to R (face 9:00), Step R Bkwd
&   Step L beside R
2   Step R Bkwd
3   Step L Bkwd
&   Step R beside L
4   Step L Bkwd

Ruby Ruby

Scatter Formation

Ruby Ruby is a 16 count 4 Wall Line Dance. The Choreographer is unknown to author.
Suggested music: I Love A Rainy Day by Eddy Rabbitt, Why Not Me by The Judds, God
Blessed Texas by Little Texas.

Step Description

Heel Touches, Steps
1   Touch R heel Diag Fwd
2   Step R beside L
3   Touch L heel Diag Fwd
4   Step L beside R

Heel & Toes Touches
1   Touch R heel Fwd
2   Touch R toe beside L
3   Touch R heel Fwd
4   Touch R toe beside L

R Vine, 1/4 Turn, Kick
1   Step R to R
2   Step L behind R
3   Step R to R while turning a 1/4 turn to R (CW)
4   Kick L Fwd

Ruby Ruby Continued

Step Description

Bkwd Steps, Stomps
1-2	Take 2 steps Bkwd: L, R
3	Stomp L beside R
&	Stomp R beside L
4	Stomp L beside R

Ski Bumpus

Contra Line

Ski Bumpus is a 40 count Contra Line Dance. It was choreographed by: Linda De Ford.
Suggested music: Western Girls by Marty Stewart, She Don't Know She's Beautiful by
Sammy Kershaw.

Step Description

Fwd Shuffles, L Break Turn
1	Step R Fwd
&	Step L beside R
2	Step R Fwd
3	Step L Fwd
&	Step R beside L
4	Step L Fwd
5	Step R Fwd
6	Pivot on R while turning a 1/2 turn to L (CCW), shift weight to L
7-12	Repeat CTS. 1-6

L Jazz Box
1	Step R across L
2	Step L Bkwd
3	Step R to R
4	Step L beside R
5-8	Repeat CTS. 1-4

Ski Bumpus Continued.....

Step Description

Toe Touches, Steps (Could be done with heel touches)
1   Touch R to R
2   Step R beside L
3   Touch L to L
4   Step L beside R

5-8   Repeat CTS. 1-4

R Kick Ball Changes, L Break Turn
1   Kick R Fwd
&   Step on ball of R beside L
2   Step L Fwd
3-4   Repeat CTS. 1-2
5   Step R Fwd
6   Pivot on R while turning a 1/2 turn to L (CCW), shift weight to left
7-12   Repeat CTS. 1-6

Slappin' Leather

Slappin' Leather is a 38 count 4 Wall Line Dance. The choreographer is unknown to author. Suggested music: Crime Of Passion by Ricky Van Shelton, Ain't Goin' Down Till The Sun Comes Up by Garth Brooks.

Step Description

R Hook
1	Touch R heel Fwd
2	Hook R across L
3	Touch R heel Fwd
4	Step R in place beside L

L Hook
1	Touch L heel Fwd
2	Hook L across R
3	Touch L heel Fwd
4	Step L in place beside R

R Heel & Toe Taps
1-2	Touch R heel Fwd twice
3-4	Touch R toe Bkwd twice

R Star, Slaps
1	Touch R heel Fwd
2	Touch R toe to R side
3	Lift R behind L and slap R with L hand
4	Extend R to R and slap R with R hand
5	Swing R Fwd across L and slap R with L hand
6	Extend R to R and slap R with R hand while turning a 1/4 turn to L (CCW)

Slappin' Leather Continued...........

Step Description

R Vine, Hitch, Scoot
1   Step R to R
2   Step L behind R
3   Step R to R
4   Hitch L while scootin' on R

L Vine, Hitch, Scoot
1   Step L to L
2   Step R behind L
3   Step L to L
4   Hitch R while scootin' on L

R Bkwd Vine, Hitch, Scoot
1-3   Take 3 step Bkwd: R, L, R
4   Hitch L while scootin' on R

Fwd Step, Fwd Slide, Fwd Step, Stomp
1   Step L Fwd
2   Slide R Fwd beside L
3   Step L Fwd
4   Stomp R beside L

Butterflies (Heel Splits)
1   Turn heels out
2   Turn heels in
3-4   Repeat CTS. 1-2

Sweetheart Schottische

Varsouvienne Position

Sweetheart Schottische is a 26 count Couple Dance. Partners are side by side in a Varsovienne Position, all facing LOD (CCW). It was choreographed by: Linda De Ford. Suggested music: Dumas Walker by The Kentucky Headhunters, Walk Softly On This Heart Of Mine by The Kentucky Headhunters.

Step Description

L Vine, Scuff
1   Step L to L
2   Step R behind L
3   Step L to L
4   Scuff R beside L

R Vine, Scuff
Man
1   Step R to R as the L hand comes up and starts turning the Woman 1/4 a turn to R (CW)
2   Step L behind R
3   Step R to R
4   Scuff L beside R, end facing partner, Man's L shoulder to center
Woman
1-3   Turn a 1/4 turn to R (CW) with 3 steps: R, L, R
4   Scuff L beside R

Sweetheart Schottische Continued........

Step Description

Vine L, Scuff
Man
1   Step L to L while starting to turn the Woman a full turn to L (CCW)
2   Step R behind L
3   Step L to L
4   Scuff R beside L

Vine L, Scuff Continued
Woman
1-3   Turn a full turn to L (CCW) with 3 steps: L, R, L
4   Scuff R beside L

Vine R, Scuff
Man
1   Step R Fwd while starting to turn the Woman a turn and a 1/2 to R (CW)
2   Step L Fwd
3   Step R Fwd
4   Scuff L beside R
Woman
1-3   Turn 1 & 1/2 turns to R (CW) with 3 steps: R, L, R
4   Scuff L beside R

Fwd Steps, Scuffs
1   Step L Fwd
2   Scuff R Fwd
3   Step R Fwd
4   Scuff L Fwd

L Bkwd Vine, Scuff
1-3   Take 3 steps Bkwd: L, R, L
4   Scuff R Fwd

Step, Scuff
1   Step R beside L
2   Scuff L Fwd

Tush Push

Scatter Formation

Tush Push is a 40 count 4 Wall Line Dance. It was choreographed by: Jim Ferrazzano
Suggested music: I'm A Cowboy by The Smokin' Armadillos, Trouble by Travis Tritt.

Step Description

R Heel & Toe Touches
1	Touch R heel Fwd
2	Touch R toe beside L
3-4	Touch R heel Fwd twice

L Heel & Toe Touches
&	Leap onto R
1	Touch L heel Fwd
2	Touch L toe beside R
3-4	Touch L heel Fwd twice

Leaps, Heel Touches, Clap
&	Leap onto L
1	Touch R heel Fwd
&	Leap onto R
2	Touch L heel Fwd
&	Leap onto L.
3	Touch R heel Fwd
4	Hold & clap hands

Tush Push Continued....

Step Description

Hip Bumps, Hip Circles
1-2   Bump R hip Fwd twice, leading with R hip Fwd
3-4   Bump L hip Bkwd twice
5-8   Circle hips twice in a CCW direction

R Fwd Shuffle, L Fwd Rock
1   Step R Fwd
&   Step L beside R
2   Step R Fwd
3   Rock L Fwd
4   Rock R Bkwd.

L Bkwd Shuffle, R Bkwd Rock
1   Step L Bkwd
&   Step R beside L
2   Step L Bkwd
3   Rock R Bkwd
4   Rock L Fwd

R Fwd Shuffle, R Break Turn
1   Step R Fwd
&   Step L beside R
2   Step R Fwd
3   Step L Fwd
4   Pivot on L while turning a 1/2 turn to R (CW), shift weight to R

L Fwd Shuffle, L Break Turn
1   Step L Fwd
&   Step R beside L
2   Step L Fwd
3   Step R Fwd
4   Pivot on R while turning a 1/2 turn to L (CCW), shift weight to L.

Fwd Step, 1/4 Turn, Stomp Up, Clap
1   Step R Fwd
2   Step L while turning a 1/4 turn to L (CCW)
3   Stomp Up R beside L
4   Hold & clap hands

Walk the Line

Scatter Formation

Walk The Line is a 26 count 4 Wall Line Dance. The choreographer is unknown to author. Suggested music: Dance by Twister Alley

Step Description

Fwd Shuffles, R Fwd Rock
1	Step R Fwd.
&	Step L beside R
2	Step R Fwd
3	Step L Fwd
&	Step R beside L
4	Step L Fwd
5	Rock R Fwd
6	Rock L Bkwd

Turn, Kicks
1-4	With 4 steps; R, L, R, L, turn 1 and a 1/2 turns Bkwd to R(CW), moving toward opposite wall. End facing opposite original wall
5-6	Kick R Fwd twice

R Coaster, Cross, Touch
1	Step Bkwd with R
&	Step L beside R
2	Step R Fwd
3	Step L across R
4	Touch R to R

Walk the Line Continued.....

Step Description

Grapevine, Touch
1   Step R across L
2   Step L to L
3   Step R behind L.
4   Touch L to L

Cross, 1/4 Turn
1   Step L across R
2   Pivot on L, turning a 1/4 turn to L (CCW), stepping R Bkwd

L Bkwd Shuffle, R Bkwd Rock
1   Step Bkwd with L
&   Step R beside L
2   Step Bkwd with L
3   R Bkwd Rock
4   L Fwd Rock

Waltz Across Texas

Scatter Formation

Waltz Across Texas is a 48 count 1 Wall Line Dance. The choreographer is unknown to author. Suggested music: I'd Love You All Over Again by: Alan Jackson, Could I Have This Dance by Ann Murray.

Step Description

Twinkles
1	Step L across R
2	Step R beside L
3	Step L in place
4	Step R across L
5	Step L beside R
6	Step R in place

Fwd Waltz Steps
1-3	L Waltz Step Fwd
4-6	R Waltz Step Fwd

Bkwd Waltz Steps
1-3	L Waltz Step Bkwd
4-6	R Waltz Step Bkwd

L Waltz Turn, Twinkles
1	Step L to L, starting a full turn to L (CCW)
2	Step R across L turning a 1/2 turn to L (CCW)
3	Step L to L turning a 1/2 turn to L (CCW), complete a full turn

Waltz Across Texas Continued.....

Step Description

L Waltz Turn, Twinkles Continued.....
4	Step R across L
5	Step L beside R
6	Step R in place
7	Step L across R
8	Step R beside L
9	Step L in place

R Waltz Turn, Twinkles (Starting a full turn to R)
1	Step R to R, starting a full turn to R (CW)
2	Step L across R turning a 1/2 turn to R (CW)
3	Step R to R turning a 1/2 turn to R (CW), complete a full turn
4	Step L across R
5	Step R beside L
6	Step L in place
7	Step R across L
8	Step L beside R
9	Step R in place

Fwd Waltz 1/2 Turn, Bkwd Waltz Step
1	Step L Fwd
2	Step R Fwd while turning a 1/2 turn to L (CCW)
3	Step L in place
4-6	R Waltz Step Bkwd
7-12	Repeat CTS. 1-6, end facing original wall

Watermelon Crawl

Scatter Formation

Watermelon Crawl is a 40 count 4 Wall Line Dance. It was choreographed by: Sue Lipscomb. Suggested music: Watermelon Crawl by Tracy Byrd.

Step Description

R Toe & Heel Touches, R Triple Step
1   Touch R toe in place, turning R toe in to L
2   Touch R heel in place, turning R toe out
3   Step R in place
&   Step L in place
4   Step R in place

L Toe & Heel Touches, L Triple Step
1   Touch L toe in place, turning L toe in to R
2   Touch L heel in place, turning L toe out
3   Step L in place
&   Step R in place
4   Step L in place

Charleston, Claps
1   Step R Fwd
2   Kick L Fwd, clap hands
3   Step L Bkwd
4   Touch R toe Bkwd, clap hands
5   Step R Fwd
6   Kick L Fwd, clap hands
7   Step L Bkwd
8   Touch R beside L, clap hands

Watermelon Crawl Continued........

Step Description

R Vine, Kick, Clap
1   Step R to R
2   Step L behind R
3   Step R to R
4   Kick L Diag across R, clap hands

L Vine, 1/4 Turn, Clap
1   Step L to L
2   Step R behind L
3   Step L to L while turning a 1/4 turn to L (CCW)
4   Touch R beside L, clap hands

Fwd & Bkwd Slides, Touches, Claps
1   Step R Diag Fwd to R with a long reaching step & bent knees
2-3   Start sliding L Fwd toward the R foot
4   Touch L beside R while straitening the knees and clap hands
5   Step L Diag Bkwd to L with a long reaching step & bent knees
6-7   Start sliding R Fwd toward the L foot
8   Touch R beside L while straitening the knees and clap hands

Hip Bumps, Heel Lifts
1   Step R in place while lifting L heel and bump R hip to R
2   Step L in place while lifting R heel and bump L hip to L
3   Step R in place while lifting L heel and bump R hip to R
4   Step L in place while lifting R heel and bump L hip to L

L Break Turns
1   Step R Fwd
2   Pivot on R foot turning a 1/2 turn to L (CCW), shift weight to L
3-4   Repeat CTS. 1-2

West Coast Shuffle

Scatter Formation

West Coast Shuffle is a 32 count 4 Wall Line Dance. It was choreographed by: Greg Underwood and Donna Nussman. Suggested music: Take It Back by Reba McEntire.

Step Description

Fwd Steps, Kick, Bkwd Step, L Coaster Step
1-2	Take 2 steps Fwd: R, L
3	Kick R Fwd
4	Step Bkwd with R
5	Step Bkwd with L
&	Step R beside L
6	Step L Fwd
7-12	Repeat CTS. 1-6

Crossing Steps (Boogie walks)
1	Step R across left (on the ball of the foot while turning the R knee to the L)
2	Step L across R (on the ball of the foot while turning the L knee to the R)
3-4	Repeat CTS. 1-2

Side Touch, Hold, Leap, Touch, Hold, Leaps & Touches, Kicks
1	Touch R toe to R
2	Hold
&	Leap onto R
3	Touch L toe to L
4	Hold
&	Leap onto L
5	Touch R toe to R
&	Leap onto R
6	Touch L toe to L
&	Leap onto L
7-8	Kick R Fwd twice

West Coast Shuffle Continued.....

Step Description

Touch, 1/2 Turn, Touch, 1/4 Turn
1   Touch R toe behind L
2   Pivot on both feet turning a 1/2 turn to R (CW) in place, end with weight on L
3   Touch R toe behind L
4   Pivot on both feet turning a 1/4 turn to R (CW) in place, end with weight on L

Step, Swivel, Slide, Stomp
1   Step R to R while swiveling R toes to R, moving to R and L toe drags along
&   Swivel R heel to R, moving to R and L toe drags along
2   Swivel R toes to R, moving to R and L toe drags along
&   Swivel R heel to R, moving to R and L toe drags along
3   Swivel R toes to R, moving to R and L toe drags along
&   Swivel R heel to R, moving to R and L toe drags along
4   Stomp L beside R

APPENDIX

A

TIME   WORKSHEET

Time (rhythm)

Name: _____

Class: _____

A. Define: Rhythm:

B. Define the following Time Signatures:

   1. 4/4:

   2. 3/4:

   3. 2/4:

APPENDIX

B

LOCOMOTOR
NON-LOCOMOTOR
SINGLE ACTION
MOVEMENTS

WORKSHEETS

Basic Locomotor Movements

Name: _____

Class: _____

A.   Define: Basic Locomotor Movement:

B.   Define the following Basic Locomotor Movements:
   1.   Walk:

   2.   Run:

   3.   Leap:

   4.   Hop:

   5.   Jump:

   6.   Skip:

   7.   Slide:

   8.   Gallup:

Basic Non Locomotor Movements

Name: _____

Class: _____

A.   Define: Basic Non Locomotor Movement:

B.   Define the following Basic Locomotor Movements:
    1.   Bend:

    2.   Bounce:

    3.   Brush:

    4.   Bump:

    5.   Clap:

    6.   Head Roll:

    7.   Hip Isolation:

    8.   Hitch:

Basic Non Locomotor Movements Continued......

9.   Hold:

10. Hook:

11. Kick:

12. Pivot:

13. Scuff:

14. Shimmy:

15. Slap:

16. Squat:

17. Stomp Up:

18. Swing:

Basic Non Locomotor Movements Continued......

19.   Swivel:

20.   Thrust:

21.   Touch

Basic Single Action Movements

Name: _____

Class: _____

A.   Define: Basic Single Action Movement:

B.   Define the following Single Action Movements:
  1.   Chug:

  2.   Cross:

  3.   Lift:

  4.   Lock:

  5.   Lunge:

  6.   Scoot:

  7.   Stomp:

  8.   Unwinding Turn:

APPENDIX

C

BASIC-STEPS

WORKSHEETS

Basic-Steps

Name: _____

Class: _____

A. Define: Basic-Step:

B. Define the following Basic-Steps:
    1. Balance:

    2. Ball Change:

    3. Boogie Walk:

    4. Break:

    5. Break Turn:

    6. Butterflies:

    7. Caribbean Walk:

    8. Cha Cha:

Basic Steps Continued......

9.   Charleston:

10.   Coaster:

11.   Cross Rock Step:

12.   Fan:

13.   Grapevine:

14.   Heel Splits:

15.   Hook Step

16.   Jazz Box:

17.   Jumping Jack:

18.   Kick Ball Change:

Basic Steps Continued......

19.   Military Turn:

20.   Military Pivot Turn:

21.   Paddle Turn

22.   Pivot Turn:

23.   Polka:

24.   Polka Turn:

25.   Prance:

26.   Promenade:

27.   Reel:

28.   Syncopated Reel:

Basic Steps Continued......

29.   Rock:

30.   Rocking Chair:

31.   Running Man:

32.   Sailor Step

33.   Front Sailor:

34.   Sailor Shuffle:

35.   Shuffle:

36.   Side Cross:

37.   Star:

38.   Step Hop:

Basic Steps Continued......

39.   Strut

40.   Sway:

41.   Tcherkessia:

42.   Triple Step:

43.   Turn:

44.   Twinkle:

45.   Vine:

46.   Rolling Vine:

47.   Syncopated Vine:

48.   Waltz (Basic):

Basic Steps Continued......

49.   Waltz - Balance:

50.   Waltz - Half Box:

51.   Waltz - Box Turn (1/4):

52.   Waltz - Half Turn:

APPENDIX

D

FORMATIONS

WORKSHEETS

Formations

Name: _____

Class: _____

A. Define: Formation:

B. Define the following Formations:

    1. Circle:

    2. Contra (Set):

    3. Couple:

    4. Couples in a Single Circle:

    5. Double Circle:

    6. Line (Scatter):

APPENDIX

E

POSITIONS

WORKSHEETS

Positions

Name: _____

Class: _____

A.   Define: Position:

B.   Define the following Positions:
    1.   Butterfly:

    2.   Buzz (Swing):

    3.   Closed:

    4.   Conversation:

    5.   Open:

    6.   Promenade:

    7.   Simple Hold:

    8.   Varsouvienne (Sweetheart, Side by Side):

APPENDIX

F

DANCE WORKSHEETS

All Shook Up

Name: _____

Class: _____

A. Time Signature:

B. Formation:

C. Position:

D. Basic-Steps:

E. Single Action Movements:

F.   Songs to dance to:

Arizona Strut

Name: _____

Class: _____

A.   Time Signature:

B.   Formation:

C.   Position:

D.   Basic-Steps:

E.   Single Action Movements:

F.   Songs to dance to:

Back in Texas

Name: _____

Class: _____

A. Time Signature:

B. Formation:

C. Position:

D. Basic-Steps:

E. Single Action Movements:

F. Songs to dance to:

The Barn Dance

Name: _____

Class: _____

A.   Time Signature:

B.   Formation:

C.   Position:

D.   Basic-Steps:

E.   Single Action Movements:

F. Songs to dance to:

Bar Stools

Name: _____

Class: _____

A.   Time Signature:

B.   Formation:

C.   Position:

D.   Basic-Steps:

E.   Single Action Movements:

F.   Songs to dance to:

Boot Scootin' Boogie

Name: _____

Class: _____

A.   Time Signature:

B.   Formation:

C.   Position:

D.   Basic-Steps:

E.   Single Action Movements:

F.   Songs to dance to:

Caribbean Cowboy

Name: _____

Class: _____

A.   Time Signature:

B.   Formation:

C.   Position:

D.   Basic-Steps:

E.   Single Action Movements:

F.   Songs to dance to:

190

Cherokee Kick

Name: _____

Class: _____

A.   Time Signature:

B.   Formation:

C.   Position:

D.   Basic-Steps:

E.   Single Action Movements:

F.   Songs to dance to:

Cotton Eyed Joe
(Couple)

Name: _____

Class: _____

A.   Time Signature:

B.   Formation:

C.   Position:

D.   Basic-Steps:

E.   Single Action Movements:

F.   Songs to dance to:

Cowboy Boogie

Name: _____

Class: _____

A.   Time Signature:

B.   Formation:

C.   Position:

D.   Basic-Steps:

E.   Single Action Movements:

F.   Songs to dance to:

Cowboy Hip Hop

Name: _____

Class: _____

A.   Time Signature:

B.   Formation:

C.   Position:

D.   Basic-Steps:

E.   Single Action Movements:

F.   Songs to dance to:

Cowgirls' Twist

Name: _____

Class: _____

A.   Time Signature:

B.   Formation:

C.   Position:

D.   Basic-Steps:

E.   Single Action Movements:

F.   Songs to dance to:

Dancin' Feet

Name: _____

Class: _____

A. Time Signature:

B. Formation:

C. Position:

D. Basic-Steps:

E. Single Action Movements:

F.   Songs to dance to:

Easy Walkin'

Name: _____

Class: _____

A.   Time Signature:

B.   Formation:

C.   Position:

D.   Basic-Steps:

E.   Single Action Movements:

F.   Songs to dance to:

Foot Boogie

Name: _____

Class: _____

A.   Time Signature:

B.   Formation:

C.   Position:

D.   Basic-Steps:

E.   Single Action Movements:

F.   Songs to dance to:

Hooked on Country

Name: _____

Class: _____

A.   Time Signature:

B.   Formation:

C.   Position:

D.   Basic-Steps:

E.   Single Action Movements:

F.   Songs to dance to:

Horsin' Around

Name: _____

Class: _____

A.   Time Signature:

B.   Formation:

C.   Position:

D.   Basic-Steps:

E.   Single Action Movements:

F.   Songs to dance to:

Lazy Shuffle

Name: _____

Class: _____

A.   Time Signature:

B.   Formation:

C.   Position:

D.   Basic-Steps:

E.   Single Action Movements:

F.   Songs to dance to:

One Step Forward

Name: _____

Class: _____

A. Time Signature:

B. Formation:

C. Position:

D. Basic-Steps:

E. Single Action Movements:

F.   Songs to dance to:

Redneck Girl

Name: _____

Class: _____

A.   Time Signature:

B.   Formation:

C.   Position:

D.   Basic-Steps:

E.   Single Action Movements:

F.   Songs to dance to:

Reggae Cowboy

Name: _____

Class: _____

A.   Time Signature:

B.   Formation:

C.   Position:

D.   Basic-Steps:

E.   Single Action Movements:

F.   Songs to dance to:

Reggae Cowboy II

Name: _____

Class: _____

A.   Time Signature:

B.   Formation:

C.   Position:

D.   Basic-Steps:

E.   Single Action Movements:

F.   Songs to dance to:

Ruby Ruby

Name: _____

Class: _____

A.   Time Signature:

B.   Formation:

C.   Position:

D.   Basic-Steps:

E.   Single Action Movements:

F.   Songs to dance to:

Slappin' Leather

Name: _____

Class: _____

A. Time Signature:

B. Formation:

C. Position:

D. Basic-Steps:

E. Single Action Movements:

F.   Songs to dance to:

Sweetheart Schottische

Name: _____

Class: _____

A.   Time Signature:

B.   Formation:

C.   Position:

D.   Basic-Steps:

E.   Single Action Movements:

F.   Songs to dance to:

Tush Push

Name: _____

Class: _____

A.   Time Signature:

B.   Formation:

C.   Position:

D.   Basic-Steps:

E.   Single Action Movements:

F.   Songs to dance to:

Watermelon Crawl

Name: _____

Class: _____

A.   Time Signature:

B.   Formation:

C.   Position:

D.   Basic-Steps:

E.   Single Action Movements:

F.   Songs to dance to:

246

West Coast Shuffle

Name: _____

Class: _____

A.   Time Signature:

B.   Formation:

C.   Position:

D.   Basic-Steps:

E.   Single Action Movements:

F.　　Songs to dance to:

BIBLIOGRAPHY

Burchenal, Elizabeth. <u>Folk-Dances From Old Homelands</u>. New York: G. Schirmer, Ind., 1922. 85 pages.

Duggan, Anne Scheley; Jeanette Schlottman, and Abbie Rutledge. <u>Folk Dances of European Countries</u>. New York: A.S. Barnes & Co., 1949. 160 pages.

Ellfeldt, Lois. <u>Folk Dance</u>. Dubuque: W.M.C Brown Co., 1969. 62 pages.

Evans, Mary. <u>Costume Throughout the Ages</u>. New York: P.B. Lippincott Co., 1950. 360 pages.

Gunzenhauser, Margot. <u>The Square Dance and Contra Dance Handbook.</u> North Carolina: McFarland & Company, 1996.

Harris, Jane A.; Anne Pittman and Marlys S. Waller. <u>Dance a While</u>. Minneapolis: Burgess Publishing Co., 1968. 386 pages.

Kirstein, Lincoln. <u>Dance: A Short History of Classical Theatrical Dancing</u>. New York: Dance Horizons, Inc., 1969. 398 pages.

Kraus, Richard. <u>History of Dance</u>. New Jersey: Prentice-Hall Inc., 1969. 364 pages.

Lawson Joan. <u>European Folk Dance: Its National and Musical Characteristics</u>. New York: Pitman, 1953.

Lawson, Joan. <u>More Soviet Dances</u>. London: The Imperial Society of Teachers of Dancing, 1965. 63 pages.

Lawson, Joan. <u>Soviet Dances</u>. London: The Imperial Society of Teachers of Dancing, 1964. 51 pages.

Lidster, Miriam D.; Dorothy H. Tamburini and others. <u>Folk Dance Progressions</u>. Belmont, California: Wadsworth Publishing Co., 1965. 342 pages.

Sachs, Curt. <u>World History of the Dance</u>. New York: W.W. Norton & Co., 1965. 448 pages.

Shambaugh, Mary Effie. <u>Folk Festivals</u>. New York: A.S. Barnes & Co., 1932.

Shaw, Lloyd. Cowboy Dances. Idaho: The Caxton Printers, 1950.

Shaw, Lloyd. The Round Dance Book. Idaho: The Caxton Printers, 1948.

Urlin, Ethel L. Dancing, Ancient and Modern. New York: D. Appleton-Century Co,, 1914.